The Tao of Twitter

The Tao of Twitter

Changing Your Life and Business
140 Characters at a Time

Revised and Expanded New Edition

Mark W. Schaefer

New York   Chicago   San Francisco   Athens   London
Madrid   Mexico City   Milan   New Delhi
Singapore   Sydney   Toronto

4 5 6 7 8 9 0   DOC/DOC   1 2 0 9 8 7 6 5

ISBN   978-0-07-184115-3
MHID   0-07-184115-6

e-ISBN   978-0-07-183935-8
e-MHID   0-07-183935-6

Thanks to Staples for allowing tweets from its Twitter page to be
reproduced in this book on page 83).

McGraw-Hill Education books are available at special quantity discounts
to use as premiums and sales promotions or for use in corporate training
programs. To contact a representative, please visit the Contact Us pages at
www.mhprofessional.com.

Contents

Introduction

When I bought my first computer many years ago, it came with two sets of instructions.

The first set was a simple color-coded poster to help you know how to plug in the mouse, the keyboard, and the monitor so you could get up and running in a matter of minutes.

The second was a hefty booklet that described the software basics, shortcuts, and practical tools to help you really make the device useful.

Studies show that about 60 percent of the people who try Twitter quit after the first week, and I'm convinced it's because they never get past the first set of simple instructions: set up a profile, follow a few celebrities, tweet about "what you're doing now," and see what happens.

Problem is . . . the second set of instructions didn't exist. Until now. And that's why we're here.

Twitter has changed my life and the lives of thousands of my clients, readers, and students. Where so many others have quit or failed, we are enjoying the benefits of the most powerful business networking system that has ever existed.

This isn't just a cute kiddie toy or chat function for keeping in touch with friends. With its real-time human-driven results, Twitter has become the networking, information, advertising platform, and search engine of choice for many business professionals. Why? Twitter can help you . . .

- Attract new audiences and potential customers, partners, and suppliers
- Follow news on your industry, market, competitors, and customers
- Find people who can solve problems quickly
- Stay on top of the latest research, opinion, insights, and competitive intelligence
- Learn new skills
- Strengthen new and existing business relationships
- Open up low-cost marketing opportunities

Sadly, most people miss this completely because they don't know what I know—and what my students have discovered.

They haven't found the path, the Tao of Twitter.

As I prepared to write this new edition, I had to reconsider how Twitter had changed, what it had become, and what it could be. As I studied the evolution of the platform and the ways people are using the platform, it was almost overwhelming to see the breathtaking creativity and collaboration that occurs when you connect people from around the world, 140 characters at a time.

Since my first version of this book, there have been four powerful new developments driving Twitter.

- Twitter has experienced explosive growth, finding new audiences among younger and older demographics as well as globally.
- It has matured into a public company with a responsibility to shareholders.
- It has developed entirely unique advertising programs that are accessible to businesses with nearly any budget.
- Twitter has become the de facto "second screen" for television, providing the channel of interactivity for live programming. This is a role that is now driving many of its strategies. It has also driven the idea of a hashtag (#) into our everyday culture! #ForReal

The first edition of this book was about the heart of Twitter, the pulse of connection that drives new relationships and tangible business results. My goal with this edition is to keep that heart intact but add some muscle to reflect the bold new opportunities for business, personal connection, learning, and fun.

If you're completely new to Twitter, I recommend that you read this book from start to finish but concentrate on Part 1, "Immersion," to get you up and running. If you're already a Twitter pro, feel free to jump around and collect some new ideas along the way.

Let's get started!

PART 1
Immersion

1
Discovering the Tao of Twitter

The first tweet I ever received was "It's 4 a.m."

Obviously, Twitter and I did not get off to a good start! Like most people, I thought it was just about the stupidest thing I had ever tried, and that first tweet seemed to confirm it.

But I stuck with it because as a marketing consultant and college educator, I was determined to learn what the buzz was about. I thought the whole thing was a little silly and maybe even spooky when unknown "followers" just started showing up.

And then I had my "aha! moment."

I was bored and was playing around on the computer one night when I logged on to Twitter and clicked on a trending topic for #NewFluName. I knew enough by this time to know that these topics represented the most popular real-time conversations in the world. Mildly curious, I clicked to see what was happening. It was a moment I'll never forget.

Remember when the pork industry was having a fit about the swine flu epidemic a few years ago? People in the industry thought the name was hurting sales of "the other white meat" and asked the public to call the epidemic something else. So thousands of people from around the world tweeted their contributions—*hilarious* new names. Like . . .

- The Aporkalypse
- Porky's Revenge
- Hog Flashes
- Porkenstein
- The Other White Flu
- Mad Sow Disease
- Hamageddon
- And my favorite, Hamthrax

Yes, it broke the monotony of my evening; in fact, I laughed until I cried! But something more important happened. I was witnessing a real-time, global brainstorming session! It dawned on me that at no other time in history could that conversation have taken place. It was an awesome moment, an inspiring moment. I began to think about all the implications for business, for networking, for problem solving, for learning, . . . and for me.

People sharing, connecting, teaching, and entertaining each other in the moment—from every corner of the world. I had caught a glimpse of something profound and wonderful.

Over the next several weeks I witnessed Twitter serve as a powerful news source during the revolutionary activity in Egypt and Iran (which put it on the cover of *Time* magazine). I made my first meaningful business connections. A torrent of links, humor, and insights came rushing at me every day as I learned to surround myself with thought leaders, teachers, and innovators. I began to realize that Twitter was probably the most dynamic, interesting, and compelling educational tool I had ever seen.

And the journey was just beginning . . .

• My region of the United States is prone to dangerous storm cells and tornadoes. As the fierce winds arrived one day, we lost power and all communication . . . except for Twitter, where I could read reports from local friends on the status of flooding and damage in the area. A tweet from a friend suggested a NOAA emergency weather center iPhone app that broadcast radio news during the storm, which I downloaded immediately.

- Through Twitter I have connected to hundreds of inspiring people from around the world, but none perhaps as loyal and dedicated as a young man named Muhammad Saad Khan, who is using Twitter and the social web to learn about social media from his home in Karachi, Pakistan. When I learned that he could not obtain a copy of my book, I sent him one. He is now using my book to teach others in his country to use social media effectively.

- A Twitter friend knew I was teaching college courses in social media and recommended me to one of his clients, resulting in a consulting engagement with the U.K. government.

- After struggling with a problem with my blog RSS feed for a week, I asked for help over Twitter and within minutes found a resource who solved the problem in one hour.

- One of my students, a music teacher, was able to promote her videos and connect to new friends associated with a well-known folk music festival in Texas. Through these relationships, she was invited to perform at the annual event. "This is my dream come true," she told me. "And it could not have happened any other way. Twitter has changed my life."

- With the help of friends I made on entirely Twitter, I created a marketing conference attended by 600 people. And oh yes, we spread the word about the event almost entirely through Twitter. Our advertising budget was zero.

I could go on for pages, but by now I hope you're starting to see the diversity, usefulness, profitability, power, and fun of Twitter.

Make no mistake; there is a Tao to Twitter. There is a majestic random synergy that holds the potential to impact your life daily—if you know what you're doing. And most people don't know what they're doing. They don't grasp the Tao.

If you dissect any successful Twitter case study, any business benefit, any personal accomplishment that started with a tweet, there is a common theme—a success formula of sorts. The more I have become immersed in the social web, the more I am convinced that this Tao, or formula, is the path to success on Twitter.

By nature, I'm a conservative person. I'm not prone to bold claims. But after witnessing thousands of people following the advice in this book and hearing their stories, I *know* it works.

Our generation's source of all wisdom—that would be Wikipedia, of course—defines Tao as a word that literally translates as "way, path, or route generally used to signify the primordial essence or fundamental aspect of the universe."

I like that idea. So let's explore this path . . . this primordial essence. But to best explain it, I need help from a young graduate student and my favorite football team.

2
The Tao of Twitter in Action

One October evening I was watching my favorite American football team—the Pittsburgh Steelers—and doing a little work-related multitasking. I flipped on Twitter and announced through a Twitter message (known as a tweet): "Watching a football game tonight—Go Steelers!"

A few moments later I received a reply from Michelle Chmielewski Belcic (or @MiChmksi, as she is known on Twitter), who was at that time a graduate student at the University of Pittsburgh. "Watching the game too! Hope we will win!" she tweeted back at me.

Now I only had a vague idea of who this person was. Although we had "followed" each other on Twitter, I could not recall ever having any dialogue with her before and certainly had no indication that this random tweet was about to change the course of our lives.

But Michelle knew who I was. Like any smart networker, she had taken care to mindfully surround herself with people she could learn from. Because I was a marketing professional, blogger, and college educator, she had included me in her Twitter tribe and now took this opportunity to reach out and connect on a very human subject—sports. She wasn't selling anything. She wasn't asking for anything. She was simply being herself, hoping to make a new friend.

About a week later I was surprised and delighted to receive an e-mail from Michelle: "It was nice getting to 'meet' you the other night on Twitter," she wrote. "I really admire what you're doing on your blog, Mark. I am just starting out as a blogger myself. Is there any way you could take a look at what I am doing and give me some feedback?"

Of course, I was happy to look at her work, and what I found astonished me. Michelle was creating innovative video blogs that were unlike anything I had seen. Her content was funny, quirky, and edgy, telling a story in a very entertaining and compelling fashion. I went through post after post, and I was convinced I had discovered an amazing talent. In fact, I had! Years later, Michelle's videos went viral, garnering more than a million views. A snippet of one of her videos was even used on a Google commercial! But at this point in her career, she was still an unknown. Now, back to our story . . .

I began to mention her wonderful posts in my tweets because I believed in what she was doing and wanted to help her get some much-deserved exposure. After a few weeks I had the brilliant idea of asking Michelle to actually make one of her charming videos for my new company. Wouldn't that be a unique way to tell *my* story and explain what I did? I was sure there would be nothing else like it.

We took an important step by moving the "weak links" of a new Twitter connection to the stronger links of a real, live phone call. I told her about my video idea, and Michelle said she was interested in the project.

She said she felt funny taking money from her new "mentor" but mentioned that she needed a new high-definition video camera to continue her work. So I offered to purchase one for her as a way to help her further her career. She picked out the camera of her choice, and my video was on its way. I was so pleased about the success that I wrote a little blog post about it to celebrate our success. I had a new company video from a Twitter connection!

Although Michelle looks back on this video as being crude compared with the wonderful art she's producing today, we both look back on our collaboration fondly. It was the beginning of a wonderful friendship . . . and we were just getting started.

The Benefits Multiply

Little could I imagine what was ahead for this little Twitter connection.

At a networking meeting in Pittsburgh, Michelle met the owner of a start-up company who desperately needed some marketing help. "I know just the guy," she told him and set up a call for me to talk with the entrepreneur.

Now I was a little too busy to take on this business, but I knew just the person who could—my friend Trey Pennington,[1] somebody I had also met through a random tweet. Just as Michelle had included me in her "tribe," I had mindfully sought out this connection with Trey, whom I regarded as a marketing mentor and teacher.

After exchanging tweets with Trey for some time, I had moved our online relationship into an offline friendship when I met him for lunch in his home state of South Carolina. During our visit he told me that the recession in his area had taken a toll on his business, and with six children to feed, he was looking for work. Trey was grateful for the opportunity and followed up with the new business lead in Pittsburgh. He had a new customer!

I explained to Trey how I had discovered Michelle, and he was also deeply impressed by her singular talent. "Can you introduce me?" he asked. "I'd like to have her on my show."

Trey produced a thought-provoking podcast called *The Marketing Professor* and soon was featuring Michelle and her innovative ideas for using video as a storytelling medium on blogs.

Between the popular blog post I had written, the podcasts, and the rush of new traffic to her blog, Michelle's star was rising fast!

As her college graduation neared, Michelle was offered a job with a social media software company in Paris. She had never had to consider a life-changing offer like this before, and she turned to me as a mentor to ask for my advice before responding.

Taking the job, she soon became a successful community manager, and her growing company needed a foothold in the United States. The company needed to hire a new business development manager. "I know just the guy," she said, and she recommended that the people at her company call me about the opportunity.

My consulting business was strong, and I couldn't take on this additional work, but I recommended that they talk to Trey, who was already on their radar screen because of Michelle. They flew Trey to London for a meeting and offered him the position.

Over the months Michelle, Trey, and I had opportunities to help and support one another in numerous ways. It could be something as important as a career choice or as simple as pinging Michelle on Skype to get help with a video editing problem.

13

Going Global

When my wife and I were planning a trip to France, we made a special effort to stay a night in Paris to meet Michelle. While it was a great thrill to finally see her in person, the visit was even more interesting because it coincided with a party she helped plan for a number of bloggers from around the world. Under a bridge. Next to Notre Dame Cathedral. With champagne and French treats!

It was a magical night as I compared notes and exchanged cards with fascinating social media entrepreneurs from Europe, Canada, Asia, and South America. One of my new acquaintances was seeking a permanent job in the United States and needed a letter of recommendation, which I was happy to provide.

I also became friends with Gregory Pouy (@gregfromparis), one of France's most outstanding marketing bloggers. Soon Gregory was translating his amazing e-books into English so that I could offer them exclusively on my blog. This provided exceptional new content for my readers and a new global audience for Greg, the beginning of a professional collaboration that has lasted for years.

The following year, Michelle left her company to become the European marketing manager for Uber, a company that created an app that allows you to connect with cabs and limousines looking for a fare in your area. When she saw in one of my Twitter updates that I was planning a trip to London, she told me she had a special app for me— free limousine service for the entire week! And with the rain we had, did I ever need it!

Can You Begin to Sense the Energy Flowing Through This Experience?

Can you see the relationships blooming, the business benefits building like an avalanche rolling down a steep mountain? And remember, it started with one stray tweet, "Go Steelers!"

It seems like a lot of luck was involved for all this to happen, right?

Wrong.

This was not luck. This exchange was enabled by the Tao of Twitter, the secret sauce that experienced social web networkers and marketers sense but may not be able to name or explain. There is an underlying wisdom that created this success story and thousands of others like it.

Let's use this fun little story about Michelle, Trey, Greg, and me to explain this formula, the Tao of Twitter.

3

The Tao Explained

I have studied, observed, and written about hundreds of different "success stories" through Twitter and the social web, and they all have one common formula running through them. This is truly the path, the way, the Tao of Twitter.

Tangible business and personal benefits are created through three elements:

- Targeted Connections
- Meaningful Content
- Authentic Helpfulness

Let's see how this works in the real world.

Targeted Connections

Today, most businesses get the idea that they need "content." But the idea of actively building an audience for it is often overlooked, and they end up disappointed, concluding that social media is a waste of time.

No amount of work, time, or dedication to marketing and social media networking will be enough if you haven't surrounded yourself with people who might be interested in you and what you have to say.

So while it might seem like the Mark-Michelle-Trey-Gregory story, noted in the previous chapter, was random, the conditions were ripe for this connection because all four of us had systematically surrounded ourselves with people likely to want to know us, learn from us, and help us.

In the next chapter, we'll go through many ideas on how to create these conditions for yourself. Networking doesn't occur by chance in the traditional business world, and it doesn't occur by chance alone on the social web either.

In the "Go Steelers" story, Michelle, Trey, Gregory, and I had *purposefully selected each other* at some point in the past, even though we had no idea what, if anything, might happen in the future. That's the majestic random synergy of Twitter that I mentioned earlier.

Think about Twitter followers as atoms flying around inside a chemist's test tube, bumping into each other randomly. Obviously the more atoms you have in the tube, the better your chances that a reaction will occur!

But every chemical reaction needs a catalyst, and on Twitter that catalyst is . . .

Meaningful Content

Content is the currency of the social web, and sharing that content is the catalyst to new relationships and business benefits.

Let's look at the role of Meaningful Content in this story. What was the content that created these powerful connections?

Tweets

Our first connection came through my simple tweet about a football game. There's an important truth here. My tweet was not a PhD thesis, a white paper, or even a blog post. It also wasn't an advertisement or a press release! It was a simplest piece of content, but it was *meaningful* to the person receiving it.

This is a lesson that is lost on many people trying to network on the social web. They offer highly engineered content aimed at certain buyer personas. And while there is value to this—in both theory and practice—networking and marketing on the social web aren't about search engine optimization, or keywords, or B2B, or B2C; they're all about *P2P—person-to-person connections.*

Social media is *social.*

There is a high value for being authentic and human on Twitter, a lesson I learned early on. Like a classic marketer, I sweated over how I wanted to "reach" my targeted audience with well-defined "messaging." But as I concocted these plans, two things happened. First, nothing happened. And second, I was bored.

At some point, I relaxed and was just me. I was friendly to people and was eager to greet them when I saw them online. I cracked a few jokes and started sharing content about something other than business—content that showed my whole personality.

At that crossroads, a wonderful breakthrough occurred. Instead of trying to find my audience and customers, they found me. *Twitter is about sharing content for humans, not search engines.*

Blogs

Blogs and Twitter fit like a hand in a glove. Twitter is the trailer to the blog's movie.

No matter how you describe it, the tweets about my blog attracted Michelle's attention, and it was this content— highly meaningful to her as a fellow marketer—that created an incentive for her to take the next step in the relationship, to connect and ask for help.

Likewise, her content (video blogs) definitely attracted my attention. Blogs can play an important role in this respect. Profiles, status updates, and résumés may *indicate* that you know your stuff, but blogs *demonstrate* that you know it!

I also used my ability to create content on my blog to showcase Michelle and her formidable video talents.

Greg's blog content earned my respect and was featured on my blog, creating awareness for him to an entirely new global audience.

Links

For the sake of brevity, I didn't get into the daily details of our Twitter relationship, but Michelle, Trey, Gregory, and I stayed in one another's orbits through interesting and helpful links we tweeted each day. These tweets linked to articles, videos, photographs—just about any kind of content that would be interesting and useful.

Other kinds of content that served as catalysts for business benefits were Trey's podcasts, Michelle's videos, and Gregory's e-books.

And finally, none of this would have happened without . . .

Authentic Helpfulness

This third and final factor is the one that is most misused, misunderstood, and simply ignored by most folks using Twitter today. This is an extremely important and subtle difference that distinguishes traditional sales and marketing from new media. I think it can be best illustrated through this next set of questions:

Do you believe that at any time in this evolving relationship my aim was to sell my professional services to Michelle? Were any of us trying to sell *anything to anybody?*

I hope you replied no, and if you did, you're on your way to understanding this very crucial aspect to the new media marketing mindset.

At least for the foreseeable future, there will be a place for cold calling and the traditional sales function. In many industries, when you schedule a call with new clients, they expect you to go through a tailored and well-rehearsed sales pitch.

But that simply doesn't work on the social web. People are sick of being sold to, marketed to, and tricked into clicking on links to unwanted products.

In an always-on, real-time, global world of business communications, the priority is on *human interaction* that leads to connections. Connections lead to awareness.

Awareness leads to trust. Trust is the ultimate catalyst to business benefits, as it always has been.

I'm going to devote a chapter to each of these three integrated elements of the Tao of Twitter. None of them can succeed independently of the other.

Before we dive into these important concepts and learn some practical applications, let's take a closer look at what we're really after here.

Why are we doing this? What are the business benefits of Twitter?

4

The Business Benefits of Twitter

In the case study I used to illustrate the Tao of Twitter, not one direct sale was made, and yet I believe you'll agree that the personal and business benefits were powerful and undeniable. They included:

- Michelle receiving feedback on her blog and videos
- A new HD video camera for Michelle
- A mentoring relationship for Michelle
- A new company video for my website
- Blog post content for Mark
- New blog subscribers for Michelle
- Podcast content for Trey
- Publicity for Michelle
- A new customer for Trey

- Job advice for Michelle
- A marketing position for Trey
- Support on video technical problems for Mark
- Invitation to Paris party for Mark
- New international blogging connections for Mark
- Global brand awareness for Gregory
- Exclusive new content for Mark from Gregory
- A work visa recommendation for Michelle's friend
- Free limo service from Uber
- A chapter for this book
- And most important for all of us, supportive friendships that will last throughout the years

And all this occurred within 24 months! Now look carefully through this list. How many of these benefits are easily quantifiable? How many could be displayed on a graph or pie chart? Almost none of them.

We need to begin expanding our minds about the possible benefits of business on the social web.

I'm spending time discussing the business benefits of Twitter because this is where most companies miss a big opportunity. They don't want to devote resources to an activity without a measurable return on investment (ROI).

And for many well-managed companies, this mindset has worked exceptionally well in the past. But if you look at the list above and other potential benefits of Twitter such as:

- Competitive intelligence
- Market insight
- A new supplier or partner
- Publicity
- Brand awareness
- An idea
- New products and services
- And yes, even a potential customer

. . . most of these benefits are intangible and difficult to display in an Excel spreadsheet! So why keep trying to do it? Many of the benefits of the social web are *qualitative*, not *quantitative*. Here's another example.

I once recognized somebody at a networking meeting from his Twitter picture. Because I had been following his tweets, I knew that he had just started a new online business, had two little boys, had recently vacationed in California, and was a baseball fanatic. I had never met him before in my life, but when I introduced myself, he gave me a bear hug and greeted me like a long lost friend! Through my stream of information on Twitter, he felt he knew me too. We had formed a connection that led to friendship and trust.

The meeting was about to start, and we didn't have time to chat, but we exchanged phone numbers and committed to meet for coffee to talk about ways we could work together. He eventually became one of my best customers.

Now how many cold calls would you have to make to find a new business connection who greets you with a . hug on the first meeting? I had effectively used Twitter to *prepopulate the business relationship!* And yes, it did eventually result in sales, but more important, it resulted in a new business connection that can create opportunities for years to come.

You Must Measure

Please don't misunderstand. I'm not saying you don't need to measure social media marketing efforts if you are using this tool for a business. Absolutely, you do. I'm an old-school data junkie, and I believe everything needs to be tied to the creation of value for the business in some way.

And it *may* be possible for you to calculate an ROI (which is strictly a financial measure). But if you *only* look at ROI, you're going to be missing the bigger picture, and you'll be left in the dust by smarter competitors.

For this reason, I think small businesses have an advantage over big companies in this space. As a small business owner, I don't find it necessary to formally calculate the ROI of Twitter (even though I probably could), because the value I am receiving is instinctive and self-regulating. I have precious little time, so I better get something important out of Twitter if I am going to devote resources to it. Like any investment in time or money, if I don't realize a benefit, I will pull back.

It gets more difficult for a larger business conditioned to run on data and not the less-spreadsheet-friendly qualitative benefits that you might be receiving from Twitter and other social media platforms. If the boss doesn't have an appreciation for this, at some point, she will wonder what all this Twittering is about and ask for a pie chart. That's when things start to fall apart.

So how do you break the ice? When benefits are difficult to quantify in discrete measures, the best way to explain the value is often through a story.

For most experienced businesspeople, hearing a compelling story of Twitter success can be just as effective as a pie chart. Once people understand how the networking operates and recognize the *range* of tangible business benefits that exist beyond just money, it's easy to make the decision to give it a chance. And once they try it, they're usually hooked!

At least that's the way it has worked for me and many of my students and customers. Why keep fretting over measuring something that can't be easily measured? Just *show* them.

Another useful tactic is the pilot program. People get nervous about commitment. Ask your boss if you can test it for six months. Then week by week, pass along the stories that show the tangible and intangible benefits as they accrue. Or perhaps they won't. Then you can kill the thing gracefully and still get a good performance review!

More Twitter Benefits

I think if you follow the guidelines in this book, you *will* see the benefits. No matter your industry or specialty, whether you're a profit or nonprofit, whether you work for a Fortune 500 company or for yourself, Twitter can absolutely be applied to the business world.

But I still observe many companies stumbling around, debating their return on investment, while their competitors are establishing a social media foothold on a business communication platform that is . . .

An Effective Promotional Tool

Nearly every study shows that among all social media users, the Twitter community is engaged and loyal. According to Edison Research,[1] 49 percent of monthly Twitter users follow brands or companies, compared with just 16 percent of social network users overall. Put another way, Twitter users are three times more likely to follow brands than Facebook users. In addition to following brands, Twitter users research and engage with companies—42 percent learn about products and services via Twitter, and 41 percent provide opinions about products and services.

Another study showed that 67 percent of Twitter followers (versus 51 percent of Facebook fans) are more likely to buy the brands they follow.

A Lead Generator

Several studies demonstrate that Twitter users more actively click on links than do users on other platforms such as Facebook. Marketing firm SocialTwist analyzed more than 1 million links on Facebook and Twitter. Facebook's shared links average only 3 clicks, while Twitter's tweets generate 19 clicks on average.[2] Another study showed that among many small and medium-size companies, Twitter users generated double the median monthly leads of non-Twitter users. That result held across company size.[3]

A Vehicle to Gauge and Express Customer Satisfaction

Service-related companies—from appliance manufacturers to the local pizza joint—are incorporating Twitter as a cost-effective and popular customer service connection. The Edison Research study showed that 19 percent of the

American social media population use the platform to lodge complaints with brands.

A Problem-Solving Tool

Here's an example of how I assembled a team through Twitter to help me solve a problem.

I have a "virtual" company. Well, it's a real company, but I don't have a building and employees and all that traditional stuff. I work with a posse of talented freelancers who might be spread out all over the country. So I have the best of both worlds. Great company, great people, but no pressure about meeting payroll every month (except my own!).

Everything works great about this model except for one thing. You can't brainstorm by yourself.

This was the problem I was facing recently when I needed to come up with creative ideas to help a client company mark its thirtieth anniversary. I had some ideas, but I've been around long enough to know they weren't the *best* ideas. For that, I needed to put some creative minds together. But how? I was on a tight deadline and needed to write a proposal quickly.

I needed some smart friends that could help me think through this problem in a pinch. And then it dawned on me! That's exactly what I had on Twitter.

This is what the social web is all about—networking, sharing, helping, creating. So with literally no planning,

I sent out one single tweet with an invitation for my Twitter tribe to join me on a web meeting at 4 p.m. that very day.

I was fortunate that seven people were able to join me on the spur of the moment, including one from Brazil and one from Spain. Some I didn't know at all; others had become my friends over months of interaction on Twitter. All were enthusiastic, helpful, and eager to try out this idea of mine!

I used an online service for the actual meeting interface and conference call. To start the meeting, I described the problem and said I was simply looking for a brainstorm of promotional options.

As the ideas were shared, I wrote them out on my shared computer screen so all participants could build on what was being said. At the end of 30 minutes, I had two pages filled with great ideas. Later that day I massaged the ideas into a proposal, presented it to company management, and—ta-da!—the company loved it! I had successfully "crowd-sourced" a promotional plan!

There were unexpected side benefits, too:

- I explained to my client how I came up with the ideas, which further strengthened the client's interest and commitment to the social web.
- The people who connected on the call enjoyed the exercise and have reached out to stay connected among themselves.

- I had an idea that worked, and it can be repeated—and is now shared with you in a book!

A Product Development Engine

My friend Fara Hain described how a Twitter search helped her discover an entirely new market for her company's product:

I admit my initial impression of Twitter was that it was pointless. But it didn't take too long to make me a believer because I saw firsthand how Twitter helped our company create an entirely new line of business.

I was pulled into the world of Twitter by two friends who were early adopters. They encouraged me to try it out and I started by "listening" through a daily search for our company on the Twitter search box. I thought it would be interesting to see what, if anything, people were saying about us. I collated responses into a spreadsheet to see if I could find a theme or locate emerging influencers.

I found that there was a group of people using my site in a completely different way than I had expected. Our company is a 3D animation company that had launched a web-based tool for teens to create greetings and videos using 3D avatars. On Twitter, our tool was being discussed with hashtags like #edtech.

It turns out we were being discussed on the podium at a major education conference! To my surprise, teachers had been using our software in the classroom as an interactive tool for students to create presentations (science classes, social studies, even a kindergarten class!). We were blown away.

By making some simple changes to our product, and asking teachers for their direct feedback, we were able to make our product more classroom-friendly. We added avatars like Albert Einstein and other historical figures and we started to be more aggressive about hiding public posts which featured less appropriate content.

In our new marketing effort, we actively targeted teachers—who are, in fact, major viral influencers—one teacher influencing 30 students is a marketer's dream!

It's doubtful that I would have ever discovered this amazing new market for our products without Twitter.

The Power of the Twitter Universe

One last potential business benefit you might not have considered: the power of Twitter users to be advocates for your products and brands.

A study[4] found that consumers active on Twitter are three times more likely to impact a brand's online reputation through syndicated Tweets, blog posts, articles, and product reviews than the average consumer!

The ExactTarget survey of more than 1,500 consumers concludes that Twitter has become the gathering place for content creators whose influence spills over into every other corner of the Internet.

- Twitter users are the *most influential online consumers*—more than 70 percent publish blog posts at least monthly, 70 percent comment on blogs, 61 percent write at least one product review monthly, and 61 percent comment on news sites.
- Daily Twitter users are six times more likely to publish articles, five times more likely to post blogs, seven times more likely to post to wikis, and three times more likely to post product reviews at least monthly compared with non-Twitter users.
- Twenty percent of consumers indicate they have followed a brand on Twitter in order to interact with the company—more than e-mail subscribers or Facebook fans.

According to Twitter, just 25 percent of its user base is in the United States. So this is an opportunity to explore, connect, and discover in an unprecedented way—whether you are connecting in a neighborhood or on a global scale.

And that's why I've spent so much space discussing benefits. Can you really afford to miss out?

Balance. Common sense. Quantitative measures when you can and qualitative measures when you can't.

Don't let your company miss out on these benefits if traditional measurements don't fit anymore. Don't get caught in analysis paralysis because you can't determine the ROI. To realize these powerful benefits, you need to master the Tao of Twitter, so let's get to it, step-by-step, beginning with those all-important Targeted Connections.

5

Tao 1: Finding Your Tribe

Many social media pundits and purists would like to have you believe that the quality of your Twitter followers is more important than the quantity. These folks are either naïve or liars. In fact, you absolutely need both quality *and* quantity.

Attracting a critical mass of Twitter followers—and by this I mean about 200 to start out—is very important as you begin your journey, for four reasons:

- First, if you have fewer than 200 people who are connecting with you, Twitter is going to be boring. And if it's boring, you're going to quit.
- Second, the more followers you have, the better the chance for a "Go Steelers" moment. The more followers, the more potential interactions; the more interactions, the more opportunities to create

business benefits. And we all *love* those!

- Research published in the journal *First Monday*[1] showed that Twitter users with more followers were more active and more successful.
- Finally, when you reach the critical mass of 200, you will start to get noticed organically, meaning you will have to spend less time following people, because relevant new connections will also begin to find you!

If you are just starting out, I strongly recommend that you spend some time up-front working on this critical aspect of your success—even as little as 20 minutes a day for a few weeks can get you started in the right direction. It might make all the difference between becoming a Twitter ninja or a Twitter quitter!

"If you build it, they will come" makes a great movie line but a lousy Twitter strategy. There's no shortcut to building a viable audience. The only legitimate method to begin to attract targeted followers is to:

1. Find them
2. Follow them
3. Hope they follow you back!

A rule of thumb is that between 50 and 70 percent of the people you follow will reciprocate, but there are five simple ideas to tilt the follower odds in your favor . . .

Five Setup Basics

Twitter success starts with setting up your profile correctly. This can easily be accomplished under Settings on your Twitter home page, which can be found by clicking the icon that looks like a gear in the upper right corner of the profile screen.

When establishing your account, here are five imperatives:

1. Always include a personal photo, preferably a friendly one. No picture = no followers. Trust me. Even if you are tweeting for a company, I would still recommend a photo of a person rather than a company logo in most cases. We are trying to establish human connections, and people relate to people, not logos, not pictures of your building, not a photo of your delivery truck. I'll cover this in much more detail later on, but aim to be *human*.

2. Include a link to your website. After all, you eventually want to drive people there, right? That's where the business gets done. If you don't have a website, direct people to your LinkedIn profile or Facebook page.

3. Create a biography with your business interests that will help people find you in searches. Add some personality! Think about the keywords people would use to find you and your business. This is important, because many apps scan Twitter bios to help discover relevant new people to follow. In an upcoming chapter, we will cover "hashtags" in depth. Using hashtags in a bio is not necessary to improve your discoverability.

4. Choose a short, easy-to-remember user name like Sally R. A name like vls767p1 is counterproductive.

5. Even if nobody is following you yet, add a few tweets. People will usually check out your profile and what you have tweeted before deciding to follow you. If you have not tweeted in a week or more, this would be a sign of inactivity and will hurt your chances of being followed back.

Are you ready now? With these profile basics in place, let's start to build an engaged tribe.

Finding Followers

"Following" people is similar to adding them as Facebook friends, except that they don't see your updates unless they choose to follow you as well. Generally the best way to get followers is to add people based on your personal interests and business synergies.

One of the beautiful things about Twitter is that you have an almost limitless ability to create your own social media experience. Unlike Facebook or LinkedIn, you can connect with people without them following you back.

Remember that it's not essential for somebody to follow you for you to realize tangible business benefits. Twitter is a great learning tool, so if a celebrity, author, industry leader, or professor doesn't follow you back, relax and just enjoy the information the person provides. In fact, most people with celebrity status don't follow back.

Once you start following someone, the person's updates, or "tweets," will appear in the "timeline" on your home page. The timeline is just a chronological record of what your followers are saying to you and the rest of the world.

By the way, if you're wondering why the system is limited to 140 characters per tweet, it's because Twitter was built to accommodate being updated from phones. The origin of the 140-character limit is based on the 160-character limit for SMS (short message service), which leaves some space for a name in addition to a 140-character message.

25 Ways to Attract Targeted Followers

If you are a new Twitter user, your first quest is to add followers who are interested in the same topics as you. Twitter doesn't really get to be fun and useful until you have a couple of hundred people in your "tribe."

Once you've exhausted your personal and professional contacts, where do you go from there?

Generally Twitter users follow a rule of reciprocity. If somebody follows you, it is polite to follow that person back. I'll cover more on follower strategies later, but the general idea as we get started is to click the **Follow** button and hope the person reciprocates.

Here are 25 ideas to build that first targeted audience:

1. Do a basic search. Start following people, companies, and brands you already know by looking for them on Twitter using the search box at the top of your Twitter screen. This way you can find existing customers, contacts, friends, and colleagues. Twitter People Search is a great *starting point* to find people that may already be on Twitter. If you can't find your friends right away, don't be frustrated. Sometimes they are listed by

their handle instead of their proper name, making it somewhat difficult to find everyone at first.

2. Choose whom to follow. Look on your Twitter profile. On the left-hand side, there is a little Twitter gadget called **Who to Follow**. Twitter looks at your followers and the people they are following, plus companies and brands you might have mentioned in your tweets, to suggest relevant people for you to connect to. It's not perfect, but the more active you become, the more accurate the recommendations will be, so keep checking back. Notice the **Refresh** button that allows you to get new batches of recommendations. Also, the first recommendation is usually a Promoted Tweet, meaning companies have paid to be in that spot.

3. Mine Twitter Lists. Once you are on Twitter for a while, you'll notice that people will place you on public "Lists." Shortly, we will dive into an entire chapter on this very useful little tool. But first and foremost, Twitter Lists are a superb way to find relevant people to follow. Lists are generally categorized by a special interest or geographic location. For example, I might be on Lists for "marketing experts," "bloggers," or "business educators." On every person's profile, you can see

a **Lists** button where you can review both the public Lists the person has created and every public List he or she is on. Once you find a relevant person to follow, dig into these Lists and you are likely to uncover a gold mine of interesting people to follow. List mining can be an addictive activity as you discover fascinating people and even more Lists!

4. Mine competitor Lists. If your competitors are on Twitter, check out their Lists and the people they are following and "steal" their contacts. Also look for Lists that follow your key stakeholders. All these Lists are public information, so there are no ethical problems with this at all.

5. Take advantage of Twellow. There are many apps that can help you find new followers, but one of my favorite places to find targeted followers for my clients and students is Twellow.com. This useful little site is like the yellow pages for Twitter. Simply sign in for free with your Twitter information, and you're ready to find and follow targeted users. It does not have a complete list of all Twitter users, but it's a pretty good start. Twellow has four useful features:

   • It has an exhaustive directory of Twitter members by every category, industry, and interest imaginable. Want to find civil engineers? Knitters? Pilots? Dog lovers? They're all here.

Results are displayed from the person with the most users to the least.

- You can also see Twitter users by city, very useful if you only serve a special market.
- You can search for people by interest *and* city.
- You can add yourself to up to 10 special-interest categories to make it easy for people to find you.

6. Search for related businesses. Do a Twitter search by your business interests and follow those who pop up in the results. They will likely look at your profile and become one of your followers. For example, if you are in construction, try searching by:

#construction

#building

#architecture

#remodeling

7. Look through other social media accounts. Connect with contacts on Facebook, LinkedIn, and other social media platforms. For example, most LinkedIn accounts now include a Twitter handle. This is a great way of finding people in your industry to follow!

8. Go hyperlocal. If you log in to http://www .nearbytweets.com, you can observe real-time tweets within a few miles of your home, even if you don't follow the people who are tweeting. This is a

great way to follow local conversations and find new connections if you are specifically building a local business following.

9. Find by "prominence." A site called www.wefollow .com enables you to find and follow new Twitter friends by their "prominence" in many career categories. The user-generated directory has lists of people who associate themselves with particular keywords and interests. An algorithm then sorts into order by what the site considers thought leadership.

10. Join Twitter chats. I've got an entire chapter coming up soon about Twitter chats, but I had to throw a mention into this list because it is such a superb method of finding relevant new contacts based on your industry or interests. Twitter chats are regularly scheduled online meetings based on special interests. Watch who is attending and then follow, follow, follow!

11. Find friends. At the top of your Twitter profile page, you will see a tab that says **#Discover**. If you click that tab, a new set of options appears on the left side, including **Find Friends**. This can help you find your current e-mail contacts if they are on Twitter.

12. Follow popular accounts. While you are still on that **#Discover** tab, check out the option on the left for **Popular Accounts**. This is not necessarily going to

deliver relevant new business followers, but it can provide access to some of your favorite celebrities, athletes, and business leaders. And who knows . . . maybe one of them will even follow you back!

13. Find activity leads. Also on the **#Discover** tab, you will see an **Activity** option. This is a very busy area, but one of the things it will display is new people that your followers are following. There's a good chance these would be good contacts for you too.

14. Link to other accounts. Link to your Twitter profile from your other social profiles across the web. On your Facebook page include a link to your Twitter profile in the websites section. On YouTube you can link to your Twitter profile in your bio and in the description section for videos. Mention your Twitter user name in your videos, or watermark it as text on top of the video. LinkedIn has a special field for your Twitter handle.

15. Add your handle to your business cards. Include your Twitter handle in your e-mail signature and on your business cards. I have links to all my social accounts on the back of my business card.

16. Tweet consistently. To attract Twitter followers, you need to be present. You're not going to attract engaged followers if you only tweet once a month. Provide value.

17. Make tweetable moments in presentations. When you give a talk to a relevant business audience, include your Twitter handle at the bottom of every slide. One popular speaking tip these days is to actually spoon-feed your listeners tidbits they can easily tweet along with your presentation. Some speakers even have short sayings from their speech in slides to encourage tweeting and new followers.

18. Live-tweet. If you are attending an industry event, there might be a hashtag for the event (more on this later). People who cannot attend the event might be following the proceedings on the hashtag. Providing relevant content from an event like this can increase relevant industry followers. Be sure to look for opportunities to engage with these new industry connections during and after the event.

19. Hold a contest. Giving away something valuable is a good way to get new people to follow you and retweet your contest to other potential connections.

20. Team up. Double your return without doubling your effort. If you've developed a promotion with another business, brand, or media partner, share content back and forth between your respective Twitter accounts. Connect and consolidate by using the same hashtag. Give followers a reason (exclusive content, discounts, insider access) to pay attention to your conversations.

21. Integrate with advertising. Many companies are displaying Twitter handles or conversational hashtags in their normal TV and print advertising to encourage new followers who might be interested in their business.

22. Use Twitter's Promoted Accounts. In Chapter 16, I'll cover an option called Promoted Accounts. This is an advertising option specifically designed to get new people to follow you.

23. Watch your followers. Whom are your followers talking about? Whom are they tweeting? Whom are they mentioning in #FollowFriday recommendations as great people to follow? ("Follow Friday" is covered in another chapter.)

24. Do an advanced search. Twitter has an advanced search function that is excellent for finding new followers by keyword and location, but curiously it is not on the main Twitter site. It's here: https://twitter.com/search-advanced. It takes a little digging to find it, but once you're there, you'll make this a go-to resource.

25. Learn to use specialized search prompts. You can unlock the basic search functionality right on the Twitter screen by learning a few of the specialized

prompts in Chapter 14. For example, if you want to find people talking about pizza in Pittsburgh, you can type *"pizza" near:Pittsburgh* and get a flow of relevant people engaged in that conversation.

Follower Strategies

Once you begin collecting followers, people will also start finding you. It can be unsettling when people from all over the world start showing up in your list of followers. What do you do about these people?

You'll see two general strategies when it comes to decisions about following people back. There is one group of "celebrities" who might have 50,000 followers but only follow a few hundred back. Comedian and TV personality Conan O'Brien famously follows only one person!

But if you're not a celebrity (and I'm pretty sure you're not), it's usually a good idea to give people the benefit of the doubt and follow them back. Here's the rule of creating relationships and business benefits through Twitter: *you just never know.*

You never know who will connect with you, you never know how they will connect with you, and you never know where it will lead (Go Steelers!).

Having said that, there is a certain element of undesirables who try to corrupt the conversation by spamming. Twitter does a fairly good job culling these folks, but Twitter needs our help too. I go the extra step and block followers who do not seem to be real people, for four reasons:

1. Your list of followers is public information and reflects on you in some small way. I want an audience to be proud of. This probably sounds old-fashioned, but I don't want to do anything in my life that I wouldn't be proud to disclose to my children. And if they examined my Twitter audience, I would not want them to see a bunch of scantily clad women peddling their videos. Anybody can see who is following you. What does your audience say about you?

2. I want to protect my followers. If I block the spamaholics, I keep them from my tweets, and I keep them, in a small way, from my friends. I see so many of these folks who copy Follow Friday lists trying to lure followers in a sneaky way.

3. I just do not want to play that game. I'm not going to be passive and imply that what they're doing is OK.

4. Blocking spammers sends a message, and that's important. But I increasingly believe that having a quality list of followers who actually exist and care about you is going to make a difference in social influence scoring models such as Klout. These systems are becoming important business tools.

How to Block Spammers

On Twitter, there are four prompts under each tweet you receive. The last one is **More**. If you click this, you will see a prompt to report a tweet. If you click that, you will get several options based on the abusive nature of the account or tweet.

How Many Followers Is Enough?

The answer depends entirely on your business strategy. As I said, you need a couple of hundred folks for Twitter to start to get interesting, but remember that you are trying to build a *relevant* and *targeted* community. The more people who follow you, the less real interaction you will have with them, so choose your "tweeps" carefully.

Let's say you are trying to connect to people who enjoy single malt Scotch in a limited geographic area. A few hundred followers may be all you need. In my business, I can sell my marketing consulting services literally anywhere in the world, so my potential audience is in the hundreds of thousands of people.

Once you get over a few hundred followers, you may need a little help keeping up with this wall of noise, and that topic is covered in Part 2 of this book, "Advanced Concepts."

The Agony of Delete

A number of people have asked me about a strange phenomenon. They observe that many people will follow them and then unfollow them almost right away. Here is an explanation of this strange occurrence, which you will undoubtedly witness too.

There are a lot of people out there who either are gaming the system by having a lot of followers or are just trying to look cool by getting lots of people to follow them while they follow few in return. They're trying to appear like celebrities who are so in demand that they cannot keep up with their fans. Perhaps this pumps up a fragile ego or maybe makes someone look like a big shot for a job interview or something. Some people may even employ automated programs to help them accomplish this.

People who ask me about this phenomenon think they are doing something wrong because so many people unfollow them so quickly. You're not. It's probably just spammers or people trying to make themselves look important, so ignore it as best you can!

A Word About Buying Twitter Followers

There simply is no shortcut to developing an effective, targeted tribe. I recently received this tweet: "Thanks for the follow. I'm gaining daily new targeted followers with www .wyz.com. It's the company everyone uses. Let me know."

While that might sound like a great idea, it's a scam called GFF, or get followers fast. No knowledgeable Twitter user would ever use these services. Unfortunately where corruption can occur, corruption *will* occur, and Twitter is no different. There is a cottage industry dedicated to building accounts of blank followers and then selling them for instant "credibility" to unsuspecting buyers.

I had a friend call me up and tell me he had just bought a Twitter account and had inherited 6,000 followers. "Now what do I do next?" he asked.

My reply: "Start over."

There are plenty of scams out there. Avoid them all. Work it the way I've described here and you *will* create business benefits!

6

Tao 2: Providing Meaningful Content

One of the most important lessons I learned on the path toward Twitter Tao was the power of content—the currency of the social web. Providing interesting content is the way to "earn" your audience.

This can also be one of the most intimidating aspects of Twitter and a major hurdle toward becoming comfortable on the channel. I once had a friend who would work on a tweet for a week before he was comfortable "publishing." And yes, you must be somewhat careful when you tweet, but it is also a historically significant opportunity to make meaningful connections and even have fun while doing it.

The subject of "meaningful content" is so important that I have divided this chapter into two parts—a regimen to get started for beginners and a deeper dive at strategic uses of content to build a personal or business brand. If you are experienced at Twitter, you might want to skip to the strategic section.

So let's ease into this. If you're just getting started on Twitter and you're trying to figure out what to tweet, you probably are saying to yourself . . .

Just Tell Me What to Do!

The key to turning a faceless follower into a real business relationship is to have a presence on the social web with relevant and interesting content. When I discussed the strategy of building targeted followers, this covered the *who* of tweeting. Now, we're going to cover the *how, what,* and *when.*

The type of messages you send out will ultimately determine your success and effectiveness on Twitter. If you are interesting and entertaining and help people with useful information, your followers will be drawn to you and also recommend others to follow you.

If you've never tweeted before, getting started can be difficult, maybe even paralyzing! But you need to become active to effectively form connections that lead to personal and business benefits. So if you are in your first few days on Twitter, here are some ideas to lower your anxiety and a regimen to get you started.

What to Tweet

The best, simplest advice I can provide is to tweet about what interests you. Although I am a marketing professional and enjoy communicating about that topic, I also love (and tweet about) sports, travel, art, technology, history, science, and many other subjects. I think that helps keep it real, human, and interesting for your followers.

One of the common complaints about Twitter is "I'm not interested in what you had for dinner." Point taken. Still, it is only human, and I think beneficial, to talk about human stuff—even eating—once in a while, especially as it relates to value-added information like a new restaurant or brand you're trying out.

The second most important advice I can provide is to get in the habit of sharing. You're already reading much of the day, right? Nearly every newspaper, magazine, blog, and video service allows you to share the content by clicking a **Tweet** button right on the page you're reading. When you read something you like, tweet it. It takes no time at all!

Here's a little system that works for me. Over breakfast each morning, I read an electronic copy of the *New York Times*. If I see a particularly fascinating article about a new social media platform for example, with a push of a button I can tweet this article effortlessly to my audience. I have just provided great, interesting content with literally no effort

. . . even while I'm doing something else. Mobile devices can also help you keep on top of content and connected during downtimes.

Finding interesting content is important to attracting and retaining followers. Be sure to efficiently "mine" content from all the sources you might connect with during the day:

- Link to your blog and other blogs—they are an obvious source of rich and relevant content.
- Link to comments you create on LinkedIn, Facebook, and other platforms.
- Tweet out an opinion about a special event, something in the news, a development in your company or community.
- Leverage your other online content. If you have something of value to offer online, like a blog, a white paper, or a website, share updates and new posts that you have written.
- Share something human. Did your baby take a first step? Did you close a big deal? Are you grateful for something today? Share it!

A Beginner's Twitter Regimen

Once you get into the tweeting rhythm, it's a lot of fun, but like anything else, it takes some practice, and it can be awkward at first. Here are some ideas to help you become a Twitter pro in less than 20 minutes a day.

- Try tweeting three times a day, at different times of the day. To start, tweet about:
  1. Some interesting non-work-related information you saw, heard, or read. *Example:* "Inspired to read in this article that violent crime is dropping world-wide: (link)."
  2. Some news related to your business, market, or industry. *Example:* "Closed on a big software deal today. A great way to start the month!"
  3. Your opinion on something going on in the news or something funny. *Example:* "Excited to watch the World Cup on television tonight. Who are you cheering for?"
- Check and respond to tweets that mention you and to direct messages at least once a day.
- Spend some time reading tweets from the people you follow. Resending one of these valuable messages is called a *retweet*, or RT. Retweet somebody at least once a day and preferably more. Select a very interesting post from somebody and pass it along to others. Remember to use this format: "RT @follower name: message." There is a little symbol that allows you to retweet right from a person's tweet. I'll cover this in more depth later.

- If it's Friday, tweet a Follow Friday[1] message for your favorite friends. It might go like this: "#FF to these awesome folks: @followername1 @followername2 @followername3."

When to Tweet

There has been a lot written about the "ideal time to tweet." But the truth is, that really varies a lot by person and the circumstances and goals. Here are guidelines about the timing of tweets:

- Tweet in the moment. No one is sitting glued to a monitor or smartphone desperately waiting for your next tweet. Twitter, for the most part, is about "the moment." So if something is interesting, timely, and relevant, tweet it as it is happening.
- Tweet in peak times. Basically, tweet during the day throughout the workweek. I know this might sound counterintuitive, but most research shows that people are most active on Twitter during business hours. If your business has international customers across time zones, think about the effectiveness of tweeting at different times of the day or scheduling tweets. Your messages will be more effective if you leave time between your tweets—at least 30 minutes and preferably an hour. If you really want to get into

the nitty-gritty details of this, several applications like Hootsuite and Buffer can help you find the optimal time to tweet based on when most of your audience is active.

- Tweet regularly. Tweet often, but *only if you have something of value to say.* You should aim for at least a few tweets a day.

- Do not have somebody tweet for you. It is becoming more common, especially among big company executives and celebrities, to hire a person or agency to tweet for you. This practice might save a little time, but it is fraught with peril. In general, be yourself.

- Thoughtfully schedule tweets. Some people like to schedule their tweets to appear at regular intervals even when they're not at the keyboard. There can be valid business reasons for this. An example would be my friend Aaron Lee (@askaaronlee). Aaron lives and works in Malaysia but is trying to build a following of business leaders in North America and Europe. Unless he stays up all night, he probably doesn't have a choice but to schedule his tweets and hope to form new connections in other time zones. He also does an exceptional job following up with people wherever they may be in the world.

The Complete Retweet

Before we move to more strategic uses of content on Twitter, let's spend a little more time on the *mighty, mighty retweet*. There are three important, outstanding benefits of the retweet, which simply means resharing somebody else's tweet. At the bottom of every tweet on the Twitter platform, you will see an option to retweet. This is a powerful gesture.

1. It takes the burden of providing all the content off you. If you have done a good job surrounding yourself with an audience of interested followers, they are going to be sharing some great stuff with you. Pass it on!

2. Sharing another's tweet is a form of a compliment. This is like saying "Great job! I liked this tweet enough to share it." This is a wonderful form of helpful engagement with the person who originated the content.

3. It puts you on the radar screen of the person you tweeted. Really want to get people to follow you? Tweet their content a few times and see what happens! They will see each retweet in their **Mention** column of Twitter. Soon, they will begin to notice you.

Here are some bonus ideas to get more mileage from your retweets:

Let's say you wanted to retweet this tweet from me: "@markwschaefer: A key to Twitter success is being authentically helpful."

The standard format (and default from Twitter) would be "RT @markwschaefer: A key to Twitter success is being authentically helpful."

However, studies show the tweet will be read and shared more often if you put the content *first*, like this: "A key to Twitter success is being authentically helpful. (via @markwschaefer)."

Why make your audience work for the content? Put it out there right up front.

To make your tweets more shareable, *keep them as short as possible*. Every time somebody retweets you, that person's name is added to the tweet. That 140-character limit is going to be used up pretty quickly, so keep it short to begin with.

Snip, Snip, Snip

A URL is the unique name used to identify a website. In fact, every piece of content on the web—a post, a video, a photo—has its own descriptor.

Problem is, most of these names are really long—quite the problem if you are limited to 140 characters to begin with on a Twitter message! Fortunately some smart people solved the problem with an application called a URL shortener or "snipper."

When you hit a **Tweet** button on an article, the URL is usually shortened automatically. But if you need to shorten a website name, this is easily done with an application such as bit.ly (no "www," just bit.ly). In addition to being a handy little snipper, bit.ly allows you to track how many people actually clicked on your link. This can be highly useful marketing information if you are trying to determine interest in an announcement, are testing different times or methods of tweeting, or want to track promotions.

Using Content Strategically on Twitter

OK, you have enough so far to get you going on Twitter. But there is a world of opportunity ahead of you to increase your number of followers, visibility, and even sales by thinking strategically about what content you share, how you promote it, and how it can engage your customers.

To illustrate this potential, let's look at three very different companies and how they used content effectively to create impressive business benefits.

Videos Create Excitement

Software provider Luxology (now part of @TheFoundryTeam) successfully built buzz and new sales for its animation software by launching it through Twitter.

To make this work, the company did not launch this product from a standing start. There was a lot of preparation, especially over the months it spent actively building its relevant, online audience of animators—the folks who were most eager to hear from the company.

But there was more to this than just following people. Luxology also consistently engaged with them to deliver value through content and build an engaged community. That way, when there was some big news to share, the company had a ready audience. This is an important lesson. Building a Twitter community takes time.

To prepare for the launch, Luxology produced some extraordinary new content—a series of new videos featuring the product. To build excitement for the launch, the company stirred the buzz by announcing its software release exclusively on Twitter. Luxology then released the new videos exclusively on Twitter throughout the launch day to surprise and delight its followers. It also pumped up the amplification of the content through Promoted Tweets, an advertising option I will cover later in the book in Chapter 16.

As the conversations built about the videos, Luxology engaged with the audience to fuel the buzz. Hours after the videos started to air, the company surprised fans again by tweeting that the new software would be available for instant purchase and use.

With the buzz created by these exciting launch videos, Luxology was able to grow its follower base from 1,700 to 22,000—an increase of 1,200 percent. The software launch was Luxology's most successful ever, with sales 70 percent higher in the first two weeks compared with its previous release. Nearly a third of the site visits on launch day were attributed to new Twitter followers attracted by the promotional content.

Sneak Peeks Build Buzz

Bob Harper (@MyTrainerBob) is a world-renowned fitness trainer and a star of the television show *The Biggest Loser*. He is also well known for his bestselling book *The Skinny Rules*. Harper had built a solid following on Twitter, and his fans enjoyed sharing snippets of content from the book and their success stories even months after its release.

When Harper was preparing to release his second book through Random House, *Jumpstart to Skinny*, the publisher decided to leverage this foundation of Twitter success by releasing exclusive content from the new book that would drive conversation, reach new readers, and invite users to share their weight-loss stories.

Before the release of the new book, the publishing team spent time aggressively building the follower base by connecting to fans of stars similar to Harper like health gurus Jillian Michaels (@JillianMichaels) and Dr. Mehmet Oz (@DrOz). The team drove engagement with this new audience by sharing relevant content related to nutrition, fitness, and weight loss.

When it was time to launch the book, Harper tweeted key weight-loss rules from *Jumpstart to Skinny* and crafted exclusive written and photographic content to inspire users to make conscious changes to prepare for the summer months. Many of these initiatives were augmented with paid Promoted Tweets.

This strategy helped drive books sales, increase fan engagement 91 percent, and gain more than 2,000 new followers.

Content Without the Budget

The two previous examples involved some pretty glitzy campaigns, but it doesn't always have to be that way. Even small businesses with hardly any budget at all can use content to create new business benefits.

My content drug of choice is my blog. But the content isn't going to work for me unless it moves—unless it ignites and is shared among my audience and beyond. Twitter is absolutely the best delivery mechanism for that content because of the nearly limitless ability to create an engaged audience. Here are some examples:

A few years ago, I received a call out of the blue from a Fortune 100 company inviting me to speak at its national sales meeting. "If you don't mind me asking," I asked the caller, "how did you choose me?"

"Our vice president follows you on Twitter," she said. "And through Twitter he became a fan of your blog. When it was time to pick a speaker, he wanted you because he loves your content."

In another situation, a Twitter follower named Tony Dowling (@MrTonyDowling) was attracted by my content (blog, video, and podcasts). This led him to buying the first edition of *The Tao of Twitter*, a book he told me "changed his life." As he followed the path of Targeted Connections, Meaningful Content, and Authentic Helpfulness, the personal and business benefits that accumulated were profound for him. He became a tireless promoter of the book to anyone who would listen.

This led to our friendship and a series of events and connections that resulted in collaboration on a new marketing conference, an invitation to speak at a European

Union think tank, a consulting job with the Bank of Ireland, the support of a European-based charity called Coder Dojo, and a workshop for the Welsh government.

All these benefits started at a single point—my tweets to Mr. Tony Dowling that attracted him to my content.

Rich Content

There is an underlying theme to these success stories, isn't there? None of these accomplishments from Luxology, author-trainer Bob Harper, and my small business would have occurred through tweets alone. It was the *link to interesting content* that drove the business results—videos, long-form written content, and podcasts.

So not all content is created equal. A link, a funny photo, a famous quote, and even a recipe or coupon are legitimate types of content, but these are not the types of content that will optimize your social media presence and bring you powerful, lasting results. If you are trying to build an effective, long-term business presence, you must have at least one source of original rich content, and you probably have just three viable options:

- A blog
- A podcast
- A video series

Only in-depth, conversational content from at least one of these sources will provide the content fuel to give you a chance to reap the immense benefits from a Twitter strategy.

There are other possible secondary sources of rich content—photographic content, SlideShare presentations, perhaps a Pinterest page—but I think the three tried-and-true sources accessible to most businesses are blogs, podcasts, and videos.

Once you make that decision and begin to execute, you'll have the content behind you that powers whatever social media platforms you choose. A source of rich content provides something that is then shareable, conversational, and engaging for Facebook, Twitter, LinkedIn, and other social platforms.

So after you have a solid business and marketing strategy in place and you are ready to embark on this wonderful social media journey, I suggest your first question should be, "What is our source of rich content?"

If you would like to learn a lot more about content strategies, you might enjoy my book *Social Media Explained*.

OK, you are one amazing content provider now. But there's still one important aspect of the Tao of Twitter left . . . Authentic Helpfulness.

7

Tao 3: Authentic Helpfulness

When somebody does something great—provides an interesting blog post, an exceptional insight, a helpful solution—I try to make an effort to compliment the person publicly on Twitter. Usually I will just tweet something like "@jfloyd helped me with a problem today. You should definitely follow Jeremy!"

One day I received a tweet from a stranger asking, "We follow each other. Why don't you ever recommend ME?"

My response was, "Because I don't know who you are! Let's change that."

It turns out this stranger was a bright young man named Aaron Killian. I had met him briefly at a speech I gave but didn't know his name, and we had never connected. Since he lived nearby, I invited him to lunch.

When we met, I discovered that Aaron was a marketing professional with a local United Way (an American organization that raises money and distributes funds to nonprofits). He told me how many charities were struggling in the tough economy, and that meant a lot of needy people were suffering, too. It prompted an idea on how we might work together.

"I've often thought that charities could benefit from using social media tools," I said. "The social web is a great place to tell a story, create emotional connection, and who better needs to get more out of its marketing dollars than a nonprofit? I've been thinking about an idea to give back to the community. What if I volunteered my time to do some training for the leaders of your charities?"

Of course, Aaron was interested in the possibilities, and after some discussions with his president and CEO, we arrived on a concept. I committed to volunteering a full day of social media training to as many people as the organization could fit in its conference center.

As the day of the seminar grew closer, it occurred to me that this could be an opportunity to create some video content for my business. When I give speeches around the country, it can be difficult and costly to arrange for professional video services. Under controlled conditions in my hometown, this would really save me some time and money. I asked Aaron if we could film the session, and he readily agreed. We were able to create two videos to promote my availability as a business conference speaker and trainer.

A few days before the event, I tweeted that I was preparing my materials for a seminar for local nonprofits. This information was picked up by a Twitter friend, Tearsa Smith (@TearsaSmith), an anchor for the local TV station. Based on the information in my tweet, she invited Aaron to a live television appearance on her morning show to promote the event. Twitter is an important source of information and leads for journalists!

I led the United Way seminar before a large, enthusiastic group, but at the end of the day, Aaron had to deliver some bad news. A local center focused on providing funding to area nonprofits announced it would be closing within the next two months. It appeared that the need to use Twitter and other low-cost social media tools was more important than ever!

To try to leverage their new skills and prepare for even harder times, the participants decided to get back together every quarter to discuss social media marketing issues. By meeting regularly they could exchange best practices and look for ways to learn together.

Several of the people decided they loved my ideas so much they wanted to sign up for my college course on social media marketing for business. Not only did they attend, but they also referred others who have now become my students, my friends, and, in one case, a new customer!

During this event, I also met a college student who became an intern for my company for the next three years.

And oh yes—Aaron finally got his complimentary tweet!

Have you been keeping a mental checklist of all the benefits that piled up from that single tweet? Quite a few!

So now let's look at the final aspect of the Tao of Twitter—Authentic Helpfulness. How did it show up in this case study?

- The fact that I was routinely complimenting and supporting other people got Aaron's attention. It made an impact on him, and he wanted to be included.
- We both wanted to meet to get to know each other better.
- By spending the time to meet him for lunch, I was turning an online relationship into an offline relationship. This is a very important part of crystallizing relationships and converting the "weak links" of social media into strong bonds that lead to business benefits.
- I volunteered my time for the seminar.
- Aaron graciously allowed me to have a video professional record the session to benefit my business.

- Participants continued to help and support one another both offline and online following the seminar.
- I subsequently offered advice and support to participants, some of whom later became my students.
- I offered paid employment to an enthusiastic college student.

There was a theme of helpfulness throughout this story. It was real. Nobody was looking to sell anything to anybody. Aaron wasn't looking to "game me"—we were authentically supporting each other every step of the way.

A Mindset of Helpfulness

I find many of the social media axioms to be dumb ("It's all about the conversation" . . . gag me), but here is one that is genuinely useful: Think of the social web as a dinner party. If somebody only talks about himself, his business, and how great he is, you're going to want to get away fast! But if a person shows genuine interest in you and offers help without regard to personal benefit, you will like that person and connect with him.

Like any business relationship, friendships on the social web are built on trust, and that must be earned.

This is the area where most people fail on Twitter, because you can't fake authenticity. If you're only out there to sell, sell, sell, people will sniff you out pretty quickly.

Recently I received this message from one of my Twitter followers: "I give up on Twitter. I have marketed, marketed, marketed on this thing and nothing has happened. I quit."

My response was this: "Your problem is that you marketed, marketed, marketed, without really trying to be helpful to people. People are sick of being sold to, advertised to, marketed to. They come to platforms like Facebook and Twitter to get away from that! However, they will interact with people, companies, and brands that truly want to help them make money, save money, save time, be healthier, be happier, solve problems, teach them something new. They interact with friends and people who treat them like friends instead of 'targets.' That is the mindset that succeeds on Twitter."

Helpful Ideas to Be Helpful

Here are some ways to demonstrate true helpfulness to others and engage in a way that *builds relationships*:

- People throw questions out there all the time. Answer them or refer the people to somebody who can. An unexpected answer is a wonderful way to delight somebody.
- Build your own tribe. Reach out to the real people on Twitter; don't just kiss up to the most influential folks. Are those folks really going to deliver business

benefits to you? Thinking that simply getting a tweet from somebody powerful is going to help your business is a myth. Build relationships. There are no shortcuts.

- Read people's profiles. Visit their websites, read their blogs, and write a comment. You can almost always find something in common with them, and this demonstrates that you are genuinely interested. And you should be!

- Nothing says I love you like a retweet now and then.

- Check your @ mentions frequently. Make sure you know who is mentioning you and try to respond to the person or acknowledge her promptly. Even with a very large following, I do my best to personally answer a question or comment directed my way.

- Show gratitude. If someone's helped you out, be sure to thank him publicly.

- Pluck somebody new out of your Twitter stream once a week and respond to a few of her tweets. You never where the majestic random synergy could lead you!

- Be genuine. Stay honest and let people see your personality.

- Take extended or private conversations to direct messages (described in the next chapter) and never have an argument in public on Twitter. Remember

that there could be dozens, hundreds, even
thousands watching this unfold.

- If people hit a milestone or have an accomplishment,
  congratulate them publicly.

- Look for opportunities to help people and answer
  questions through links to your blog posts, videos,
  and other helpful content. This is an excellent way to
  be helpful and drive a little traffic to your site at the
  same time.

- If a friend in your audience seems to be struggling
  or suffering, offer to get on a phone call or Skype to
  help the person.

- If you are attending a speech, workshop, or panel
  discussion, "live-tweet" highlights from the talk with
  the presenter's handle. This is a wonderful way to
  promote the presenter and the presentation with
  your audience.

- Use every opportunity to extend the conversation
  and the relationship by taking it offline. Connect
  in a deeper way through e-mail, a phone call, or a
  live meeting. Converting weak links to strong links
  accelerates the opportunity for meaningful personal
  and business benefits.

Being genuine and helpful sounds so easy doesn't it?
But of the three aspects of the Tao of Twitter, this is the

one that is most easily overlooked and abused by business professionals trying to fit the old "broadcast" mode of communicating into this new format.

A Case Study in Authentic Helpfulness

Here is one of my favorite examples of Authentic Helpfulness in action. About two years ago, I received this e-mail from a complete stranger:

> Mark,
>
> I was inspired by your book "The Tao of Twitter" and wanted to practice Authentic Helpfulness. I decided to do a few Twitter background pages for you that are based on the feel of your book cover.
>
> I'm happy to make tweaks or revisions if it's close to what you want but not exactly. Feel free to use or not—it was a fun exercise to try.
>
> Thanks so much for your insights. They reinforced a lot of how I have approached Twitter and provided some new ideas to try.
>
> Carl Brand

Carl, who goes by @MyVogonPoetry on Twitter, has become a friend. I was so blown away by this gesture that I wrote a blog post highlighting his act of generosity (while also promoting his business). He has subsequently created a beautiful background for another of my books, *Return on Influence*, and we continue to enjoy each other's company on Twitter. He may also be the funniest man I know! Who knows where it will lead?

Scaling Helpfulness

If you are working for a larger company, you might be thinking at this point, "Yeah . . . how are we supposed to do this in a practical way when we have thousands of customers?"

Let me start with a quote from an intellectual hero of mine, Dr. Robert Cialdini, the well-known author of *Influence at Work*. I had the honor of interviewing him one time and asked him, "In a world of increasing information density, how is it possible for a company to stand out?"

His answer was simple and profound: "Be more human."

I believe in this and think if you study marketing, advertising, and culture, you'll find that we are seeing a renaissance in design, products, and messages that emphasize a human touch.

And yes, Authentic Helpfulness can scale:

The Hilton Hotel chain has an account called @HiltonSuggests that plucks traveler questions from Twitter and helps answer them—even if the questioners are not staying at a Hilton. The account might help with a restaurant recommendation, entertainment in the area, or even directions.

Staples, the office supply megachain (@staples), engages with customers in real time. Each tweet ends with an employee's initials so you know there is a real person behind the message.

The Bank of Ireland (@bankofireland) also has employee initials after every tweet, and its tweeters routinely have online conversations with customers about current events, shopping, entertainment, and local sports.

Chili's restaurant chain (@chilis) routinely monitors customer tweets and tries to respond to tweets while the customer is still sitting in the restaurant.

Chobani Yogurt (Chobani) is known for its responsive and friendly banter on Twitter. When the company changed its serving size (an unpopular move with many loyal customers), it personally responded to every tweet. And if you engage with this company, don't be surprised if you randomly get some free product sent your way!

General Electric (@generalelectric) recently sent pies to 314 Twitter followers on "Pi Day"—March 14. Why? The company said it was trying to throw back the curtain on the company and show its humanity in an effort to connect to young people who love technology. It is trying to increase awareness about its many products beyond lightbulbs and appliances.

FinnAir (@finnair) built an entire community of "Quality Hunters" who scoured the world for air transportation and hospitality best practices. This created a highly engaged and loyal fan base as the airline implemented suggestions and rewarded its customers.

These are just a few diverse examples of how even large companies are creating a helpful, human presence that leads to awareness, connection, and loyalty.

Now that we've walked through the three fundamental aspects of the Tao of Twitter, let's start putting it into action!

8

Unraveling Twitter

If you follow the path of Targeted Connections, Meaningful Content, and Authentic Helpfulness, you will have an enormous competitive advantage over those who might take months or years to understand these lessons—if they ever learn them at all.

But even with this knowledge, Twitter can be daunting. It has its own language and vibe. People toss around terms like "hashtags," "Twitter chats," "#FF," and so many quirky acronyms that it can make your head spin. It can be a bit like entering a foreign country!

In this chapter I'm going to cover some ideas to help you get on the fast track, speed your learning curve, and gain a competitive edge in the Twitter universe! Let's cover:

- The language of Twitter
- Getting the most from your tweets

The Language of Twitter

Learning some of the common terms and acronyms is one of the most important things you can do to put yourself at ease. In fact, the confusing language of Twitter is one of the primary reasons people quit!

If you're already a Twitter pro, you'll be familiar with the ideas in this section, but if you're new, this is going to help a lot! Here are a few of the most common terms and designations you will encounter:

@ reply. The @ sign is used to indicate that you are replying to a specific user name. For example, if your friend Jim Smith tweets a question asking about the best place to buy a Jeep, you will reply with "@ JimSmith (or whatever the handle is) I have one for sale, come on over." Remember that when you use "@reply," it is visible to everyone—even people who don't follow you.

Avatar. An avatar is the personal image uploaded to your Twitter profile in the **Settings** tab of your account.

BFN. This acronym is shorthand for "Bye for now."

Block. The act of blocking keeps a particular Twitter

user name from following you and your tweets. You block someone by clicking on his or her profile and choosing **Block** in the settings.

Block and report. Twitter also gives you the opportunity to block somebody and, if you think the person is doing something offensive or illegal, to report him or her to the service. After a few reports like this, the person can be suspended from Twitter.

There are several different ways to block or report somebody, but the easiest way is to go to your list of followers and find the offensive account. Beside every account, you will see buttons that will allow you to follow people or create other actions. If you click on the icon that looks like a person, you can block the person, report him or her, or take other actions.

Blocked users cannot:

- Add your Twitter account to their lists
- Have their @replies or mentions show in your **Mentions** tab (although these tweets may still appear in a search)
- Follow you
- See your profile picture on their profile page or in their timeline

Direct messages, or DM. This is the Twitter equivalent of
private e-mail. You may only send direct messages
to those you follow and who are also following
you. Depending on how you are accessing your
tweets, there are a number of different ways to send
somebody a direct message. The easiest way is to
access the **person** icon described above and click
Direct Message.

To view messages sent to you, on your Twitter
profile, click on the **envelope** icon on the top right of
the page.

EM. This acronym is shorthand for "e-mail me."

Favorites. One of the options you will see on every tweet
you receive is a **Favorite** link. If you click this, it will
store the tweet in your Favorites for future reference.
This is a handy tool if you want to come back to
something at a later time. To see your favorite
tweets, click on the **Me** icon at the top of the profile
and you will see a prompt on the left for Favorites.
Note that if you have a public account, everyone has
access to your Favorites.

Feed. Your posts on Twitter are commonly referred to
as your "Twitter feed" or "timeline."

Follow. To follow people on Twitter means to subscribe
to their tweets or updates on the site. You do this by

clicking the **Follow** button on their profile. Clicking it again will "unfollow" them.

Follow Friday, or #FF. It is a tradition to recommend your favorite followers every Friday. This is a polite way of thanking people who have done a good job or did something special to help you during the week. A typical format might be "#FF @uscr1 @ uscr2 @user3 for their great content this week!"

HT. A "hat tip" is usually followed by someone's Twitter user name. Using HT means you aren't quoting or retweeting the person directly, but instead acknowledging that she gave you the idea for the content you're tweeting.

ICYMI. This acronym for "in case you missed it" can be used when someone is tweeting about big news or a trending topic a few days after the fact.

IDK. This is shorthand for "I don't know."

IMO or IMHO. You'll usually see "in my opinion" or "in my humble opinion" when someone wants to agree or disagree with a piece of content he's sharing.

Locking. You can "lock" your profile so that only friends can see your updates by clicking on the gear at the top right corner of your profile and then clicking on **Settings**. Locking your account would certainly *deprive you of followers* who would have otherwise followed you if they could see your tweets. After all, you're trying to network, right? Since you're reading this book to build business connections, I would strongly recommend that you keep your Twitter feed open and available to anyone who wants to interact with you.

Mentions. Any time somebody uses the @ symbol with your Twitter name (also called handle), it will show up in your list of mentions, which is displayed if you click the @Connect button at the top of your Twitter home page. This function is extremely important to monitor every day to see who is mentioning you in their tweets. Look for opportunities to engage and help people who are mentioning you by name.

MT. This means "modified tweet" and is used to let people know you changed the original tweet. For example, sometimes you have to change a tweet slightly to make it short enough to fit the 140-character limit. This is generally acceptable as long as you don't change the meaning of the tweet. It is polite to signify the change by putting "MT" at the beginning of the tweet.

Promoted Accounts, Trends, Tweets. Twitter is finding innovative ways to capitalize on its popularity and monetize its service without impeding users. One way it is doing this is by allowing brands to sponsor

tweets and topics that are trending. Any tweet or
promotion is supposed to be clearly marked as
advertising or "promoted." This is covered in detail
in Chapter 16 in Part 2 of this book.

Recent images. An application on your Twitter profile
page shows recent images you have somehow
interacted with—images shared through mobile
uploads, images you have tweeted (or retweeted
from others), images you have commented on, and
so forth. Your only option to get these out of your
recent image gallery is to delete the tweet associated
with the image. You can do this if you click on
a recent image and then the **Delete** link under
the tweet.

RT, or retweeting. RT stands for "retweet," meaning a
"resent" message from someone else's Twitter post.
If you see "RT," this means it is not the sender's
original content—it came from the person listed after
the RT designation. Another way to credit people
for content or a link is to put "via @username" at the
end of the tweet. There are many variations on this
theme, but the main point is, it's polite—and good
business—to credit others for their work.

Search. This is located at the top of your Twitter home
page. This is a powerful tool for finding people,
links, and the latest real-time news. There is also

an advanced search tool and other search tips we'll cover later on.

TFTF. You always want to say thank you, so "thanks for the follow" is a nice way to recognize that someone has decided to add you to her Twitter feed.

TMB. This is shorthand for "tweet me back."

Trends or Trending Topics. Located in the left-hand column of your Twitter home page, this list indicates the most popular topics in real time. This is an effective and entertaining way to see what people are saying about a subject in the moment, anywhere in the world. You will see tweets from anybody tweeting on a topic, not just your followers. Often, the topic at the top of the list is "sponsored," which means a company paid for that placement.

Tweeps, tweeples. Both terms refer to a cluster of friends on Twitter. They're frequently used to address all your followers at once, e.g., "Morning, Tweeples!" The Twitter world will try to force any kind of descriptive word into a format that begins with "Tw" unfortunately. Another common example is the . . .

Tweetup. Twitter folks are very loyal to each other, and they love to meet in real life (IRL) at social gatherings called tweetups. Tweetups may be formally scheduled as part of a meeting or conference or happen on the spur of the moment.

The social side of social media! They can be great
networking events.

Making the Most of Your Tweets

In the social media world, there is a lot of published
research, but there is not a lot of *valid* research.
Unfortunately, surveying a bunch of blog readers and then
posting the results as "research" is all too common today.

But a few years ago, my friend Dr. Ben Hanna led an
extensive statistical study to discover the optimal tweeting
strategy, and I think his findings stand up as some good
parameters for getting the most mileage out of your tweets.
Here are four key findings.

- Tweet quality versus tweet quantity. The study
  looked at the relevant importance of tweeting
  only when you had something really interesting to
  pass along (quality focus) versus tweeting more
  frequently (quantity focus) for building a Twitter
  following. The study showed tweet quality is *much*
  more important than quantity: the higher the
  average number of clicks per tweet with a trackable
  link in a given week, the higher the follower growth
  (controlling for total number of followers). However,
  tweeting consistently also matters. The average

tweets per day of the most successful accounts ranged from 2.9 to 11.0 per day.

- The importance of the first words. At 140 characters, tweets are like headlines, and people skim them quickly. If you want to catch someone's eye, think like a headline writer and make sure the main-topic keywords or a number or statistic is found in the first three to five words. If you are retweeting, put the author's name at the end of the tweet, not at the beginning.

- The average lifespan of a tweet. If you measure the lifespan of a tweet by the number of days on which it receives at least one click from a Twitter user, then business tweets don't live very long. On average, tweets with a clickable link received at least one click on 4 separate days, with a range of 1 day (not a very popular tweet) to 23 days (very popular content).

- The optimal time between tweets. In a study examining the number of clicks on business-related tweets, the optimal space between business tweets to attract the most clicks is either 31 to 60 minutes or 2 to 3 hours. Tightly packed tweets just don't appear to attract as much attention as tweets with more space between them. The cause of the dip in click activity for tweets between 61 and 120 minutes is uncertain.

Many Twitter applications allow you to schedule tweets so you can distribute your content throughout the day even if you are occupied.

There is one more term you should know to be fluent in the language of Twitter. It throws a lot of people off but might just be the single greatest innovation on this social media platform—hashtags!

9

#Hashtag-mania

There is probably no aspect of Twitter that is more misunderstood, discussed, and abused than hashtags. And arguably, the inclusion of hashtags as an easy way to group tweets is the most important innovation in the history of Twitter, perhaps the history of social media. It seems like such a small thing, but hashtags are the key to making sense of Twitter—and sometimes the key to making money on Twitter.

On August 23, 2007, the Twitter hashtag was born. Invented by Chris Messina (@chrismessina), the first tweet with a hashtag was "how do you feel about using # (pound) for groups. As in #barcamp [msg]?"

According to an article in gigaom.com,[1] the inspiration did not take off for quite a while. "In the beginning people really hated them," Messina said. "People didn't understand why we needed hashtags, and the biggest complaint was that people just didn't like how they looked."

Messina pitched his hashtag idea to Twitter's execs, but the Twitter team deemed the hashtag too nerdy.

Adoption of the hashtag lagged until October 2007, when people tweeting about forest fires in San Diego started using the same hashtag on each tweet so news about the event was more easily searchable. Later that year, hashtags were adopted by some political campaigns, and the tradition caught on quickly from there.

Today hashtags make tweets more meaningful and discoverable. No conference or speech is complete without a hashtag these days, connecting participants, presenters, and people who might be following the proceedings over Twitter from anywhere in the world. Hashtags are a foundation for monetization, for curation, for movements, for memes, and for fun.

According to Twitter, 11 percent of tweets now contain hashtags. Because of the public, quick, and in-the-moment nature of Twitter, hashtags have helped define the channel, although Facebook and other platforms have tried to copy it.

10 Useful Insights About Hashtags

There are endless ways to use hashtags to group news events, ideas, and conversations, but here are 10 interesting ways you can begin using hashtags in your daily Twitter life.

1. Discussions and Chats

Some people will designate a hashtag to group all messages from an extended conversation. The best example of this is using hashtags for topical Twitter chats, which we will cover in the next chapter. So for example, if you wanted to see everything that was being said in a weekly chat about nursing topics, you could type #nursechat into the Twitter search box to see commentary from around the world.

2. Discovery

Let's say you are tweeting a link about an automotive marketing trend you're excited about. The title of the article may not contain the word "automotive" or "marketing," but by including both words at the end of the tweet like this: #automotive #marketing, it will help other people looking for those topics find you and your content. Choosing the right hashtag can help amplify your message.

3. Trending Topics

The biggest conversations in the world are grouped by hashtag and displayed on Twitter as Trending Topics. This is a very popular way to keep up with real-time, global conversations.

4. News and Emergencies

If you want your tweet to reference a certain news or community event, hashtags can be very useful. It was probably no accident that hashtags first caught on to curate news about a tragic wildfire. When a flood hit Nashville a few years ago, the power was out, and so people could not access local news. My friend Laura Click (@lauraclick) lived through the disaster and reported that the only way people could follow the news and get emergency assistance was by following the #NashvilleFlood hashtag on Twitter.

5. Contests and Promotions

Encouraging people to tweet about your business and a hashtag to win a prize has become a very popular way to gain exposure and new followers for a business.

6. The Second Screen

Studies show that the majority of people watching TV today are interacting with social media at the same time . . . and most of that is occurring on Twitter. Twitter has become the de facto "second screen" for TV and has been particularly important for live events. For example, during the National Hockey League's televised Winter Hockey Classic, the network encouraged people at the event to tweet photos from the game under the hashtag #WinterClassic. The photos were used during the broadcast and on the network's web properties. Many live entertainment, sports, and news programs incorporate live tweets into their programs that are culled from hashtags.

7. Research

I was planning a trip to the lovely city of Copenhagen. I had never been there before and was at a total loss about what to see, what to do, and what was hot. When I entered #Copenhagen into the search box, I received a wealth of interesting insight, including:

- Discussions about hot new restaurants
- Photos from several art gallery exhibits
- A music festival that was occurring when I was in town
- A new article about the architectural highlights of the city
- A photo essay on the "contrasts of Copenhagen"
- Comments about the long security lines at the airport
- A blog post about favorite Copenhagen pubs

This is different from a Google search because you get news and conversations happening right now.

There are obvious benefits for companies and brands that learn how to use Twitter for real-time research. One marketer told me he considered Twitter the greatest source of marketing insight he had ever seen.

You can also save Twitter searches so you can see an interesting stream every day about #Copenhagen, your competitors, conversations about your products, or anything else you are interested in.

8. Creating Buzz

If you are planning an event, product launch, or special announcement, start using a hashtag in your communication activities as you approach the big day. It will raise curiosity and prompt people to search for other tweets using that hashtag.

9. Silliness

Perhaps the most popular use of hashtags is to simply be funny. Twitter has opened up a whole new world of humor, collaborative writing, and word play. To show you an example of how this works, a group of friends might pick a challenge hashtag and then dream up the funniest content to go with it. Here are some examples from one my favorites, Carl Brand, who can be found at @MyVogonPoetry on Twitter:

- I like big buttes and I cannot lie. **#TravelSongs**
- Ebony and "She's Touching Me!" **#TravelSongs**
- Things can only get wetter. **#TravelSongs**
- Talk Yahtzee® to me. **#BoardGameSongs**
- I would die 4 Clue® **#BoardGameSongs**
- Baby got Backgammon. **#BoardGameSongs**
- Peter Pandemic. **#ZombiesOnBroadway**
- Man I'm La Munchin. **#ZombiesOnBroadway**
- Glengary GlenGross. **#ZombiesOnBroadway**

10. Newsjacking the Hashtags

There are several clever examples where brands or individuals have inserted their own tweets into a Trending Topic to create massive brand awareness. When NBC broadcast a live performance of *The Sound of Music* on American television, a massive audience tweeted along by following the hashtag #TheSoundOfMusicLive. Then DiGiorno Pizza got involved, creating whimsical tweets right along with the performance:

> #TheSoundofMusicLive Can't Believe Pizza Isn't One of Her Favorite Things
>
> DOUGH a crust an unbaked crust. RAY a guy that likes pizza. ME a pizza liked by a guy named Ray. FAH no idea what fah is. #TheSoundOfMusicLive

Millions of people were following the show's hashtag, and the dozens of DiGiorno tweets caught on and went viral.

Corrupting Hashtags

Hashtags are like little beacons attracting people to your content. In the case of DiGiorno, it worked to attract massive, positive awareness for very little effort. But hashtags can also attract the wrong kind of attention.

For several years I led a popular conference called Social Slam. When you have 600 frenzied tweeters pumping out reports under the #SoSlam hashtag, it gets some attention. In fact, we "trended" on Twitter every year. About two hours into the conference, I started seeing people with no association with the conference begin to tweet ridiculous stuff—ads for pornography, promotions for local businesses, even people who were pretending to be at the conference but were 1,000 miles away.

Because the hashtag was trending, we had attracted a huge number of people who were following the conference proceedings from afar. The spammers had hijacked the hashtag to insert their own trash. At its peak, about one out of every five conference-related tweets was coming from spammers!

I don't want to scare you off at all. It's unlikely that any hashtag you use for your event is going to have any problem unless it is generating thousands of tweets. But I just want you to be aware of the whole story on hashtags.

I hope this chapter has provided a helpful glimpse of the many creative uses of hashtags. Let's turn to another useful innovation: Twitter Lists.

10

Lists—the Key to Twitter Sanity

It's easy to lose sight of real connections when you're first confronted with the wall of noise that is Twitter. Especially in the beginning, when you are hitting **Follow, Follow, Follow** or reciprocally follow everyone who is following you, it is easy to get confused in a rising tide of new followers. You are going to be losing a lot of great information from people you care about if you don't get it under control.

Twitter Lists offer an elegant way of solving that problem. You could follow someone else's prefab Twitter List. You can find a list of must-follow tweeters on just about any topic under the sun: dog groomers, pilots, marketing gurus, business leaders in Philadelphia, Atlanta food trucks.

And following Lists like these offers an easy way of quickly getting a taste of a whole bunch of different people and finding out whom you're really interested in, without making a big commitment; unlike following people one by one (which can make it tough to prune the number of people you follow when it grows too big), you can follow and unfollow everyone on a single Twitter List with just a click.

But the real power of Twitter Lists comes from creating your own public or private Lists to keep your stream manageable and fun.

As you get into the flow of Twitter, you'll probably find yourself naturally grouping people in your mind. Customers. Competitors. My online friends. People I admire. Twitter Lists allow you to organize the Twitter stream so you can make sense of what might seem like chaos.

By clicking on the **Me** icon at the top of the Twitter profile, you can get started using this essential utility for monitoring the tweets from smaller groups of people who are important to you.

Notice when you click the **Lists** tab on your profile, you'll see two options in the center of your screen for Lists **Subscribed to** and Lists **Member of.** This is going to sound weird, but since Twitter went through a redesign a few years ago, it is impossible to know how many Lists you are on unless you manually count them! The only quick way I know to instantly see how many Lists you are on is to subscribe to either Hootsuite or TweetDeck and then click on your name in a tweet. When your profile pops up, it shows how many times you have been listed.

The Basics

To create a list:[1]

1. Go to your **Lists** page. This can be done by clicking the **gear** icon drop-down menu in the top right navigation bar or by going to your profile page and clicking on **Lists**.
2. Click **Create list**.
3. Enter the name of your list, add a short description of the list, and select if you want the list to be private (only accessible to you) or public (anyone can subscribe to the list).
4. Click Save list.

Note: List names cannot exceed 25 characters, nor can they begin with a number.

To add or remove people from your lists:

1. Click the **gear** icon drop-down menu on a user's profile.
2. Select **Add or remove from lists.** (You don't need to be following a user to add that person to your list.)
3. A pop-up will appear displaying your created lists. Check the lists you would like to add the user to, or uncheck the lists you'd like to remove the user from.

4. To check to see if the user you wanted to add was successfully included in that list, navigate to the **Lists** tab on your profile page. Click the desired list; then click **Members**. The person should appear in the list of members.

To edit or delete lists:

1. Go to your profile page.
2. Click on the **Lists** tab.
3. You will see lists you've created and other people's lists you follow under **Subscribed to**.
4. Select which list you'd like to edit or delete from the lists you've created. Click **Edit** to update your list details or click **Delete** to remove the list entirely.
5. You cannot add or remove people from your list on this page—you must do that from the profile pages of each person you wish to add or remove.

To subscribe to or follow other people's lists:

1. Click on **Lists** when viewing someone's profile.
2. Select which list you'd like to subscribe to.
3. From the list page, click **Subscribe** to follow the list. You can follow lists without following the individual users in that list.

Seven Ideas to Help You Master Lists

Lists are very important as a personal productivity tool, but they also can help you with your business in many ways. I've already discussed their crucial role in finding targeted followers. Here are some additional ideas to leverage your public lists in creative ways:[2]

1. Share Your Lists on Other Platforms

Most people share their lists within Twitter. But don't stop there. Plan on sharing the links to your lists on your website or blog. To find a List's URL to share:

1. Go to the list you'd like to share.
2. Copy the URL that shows up in your browser's address bar. It will look something like this: https://twitter.com/username/lists/list_name.
3. Paste the URL into a message, newsletter, Facebook post, or anywhere else you want to share the list.
4. Here is a fun list that I will share with you! Would you like to follow every person mentioned in this book with one click? This is your lucky day. I have created a "Stars of Tao" list just for you. Follow this link, click **Follow**, and all these great people will now in your Twitter Tribe: http://bit.ly/taostars

2. Include Yourself in Your Lists

Actually, it's not so obvious how you go about adding
yourself to your own Twitter List, even though there are
lots of reasons to do so.

Why would you put yourself on your own list? If you do
a good job curating your lists, many people may want to see
who is there and follow them—or perhaps even follow the
whole list. Why not include yourself so you're followed too?

Believe it or not, Twitter does not allow you to add
yourself to your own lists, so you need some help from
Hootsuite (also a free application). All you have to do is open
your own profile (by clicking on your own user name in a
tweet that mentions you) and then click **Add to list**. Select
the List you want and voilà! It's that easy.

3. Name Your Lists Well

You'll give your Lists names, and those names will be
part of a shareable URL. Choose a name that is enticing
and accurate, such as "My Favorite Bloggers" or "Metals
Industry Experts."

4. Create Lists Helpful to Your Target Audience

Think of Lists as a marketing tool. Ask yourself these
questions (bloggers, replace "customer" with "audience"):

- Who are my target customers?

- Do they fall into distinct segments with different needs or interests? If so, define each customer segment.
- What are their goals, as they relate to my area of business?
- What kind of information helps them reach those goals?
- What kind of information is this type of customer generally interested in?
- Who on Twitter regularly tweets that kind of information?
- What Twitter resources can be valuable to this customer segment, given these customers' goals?

Now, using the answers to that last question, create one or more Lists for each customer segment designed to meet the customers' goals. For example, let's say you're a realtor. You'd like to attract potential home buyers in the Chicago area. You might decide that the key customers you want to attract are first-time home buyers and people thinking of selling their homes. You come up with this list of information goals for first-time buyers:

- Information about the home-buying process
- Information about mortgage types, qualifying, and so on

- Tips for home shopping
- Information about what to look for in walk-throughs, inspections, etc.
- Tips for deciding what you want in a house
- Information about neighborhoods, amenities, schools, etc.
- Real estate market and interest rate trends

Based on this List, you're able to find several bloggers and home magazines on Twitter that tweet about home buying, loan types, the home-buying process, etc. You find some good Twitter sources for mortgage and interest rate information. You find several Twitterers who tweet about Chicago neighborhood statistics or tweet links to articles and blog posts about neighborhoods, and so on. And you add all these sources, and yourself of course, to create your "Chicago First-Time Home Buyer" List.

Remember, these Lists can also be followed by competitors! Be aware of the competitive environment.

5. Make Employee Lists

You might have a link to your Twitter account on your website, but don't forget to make an official employee Twitter List. You should include all official company accounts, along with employees who tweet on behalf of the organization (or if you have a more open culture, you could include any employee who tweets). Creating a Twitter list of employees is also a good way to see what everybody is up to!

6. Use Lists to Create Minicommunities

Let's say you blog about parenthood, or you're a retailer that sells products for new and expecting parents. *Why not build a community that also aligns with your business needs?*

Create a list for expectant parents on Twitter. Make the initial list from whoever you know is expecting; then invite others to join your list. Spread your invitation far and wide on Twitter, your website, Facebook, etc. Expectant parents can send a message to you to get added to the list. Ask the List members to nominate other expectant parents on Twitter. Keep spreading the word until you hit the 500 List-member limit.

Now, you've created a minicommunity consisting of your target market. It's a great resource for the List members and provides a real service to them. It's a place they can go to view the tweets of other expectant parents, kind of like a chat room. In the process, you've met a whole bunch of new potential customers that you can now get to know and share your products with.

7. Develop Political Campaign Lists

Running for office? Aggregate your supporters or "friends of" the campaign for increased visibility. It's important to stay connected to constituents, especially during election time (every vote counts!).

If you're a political reporter or blogger, create a private list of all the candidates you're tracking to keep tabs on their tweets more easily. (This same principle could be applied by journalists or bloggers to any beat, not just politics.)

* * *

Well, by now I hope you're starting to get a little more comfortable and confident in the language and workings of the Twitter platform. And of course, you're constantly working on your Tao: connections, content, and helpfulness.

But wait a minute . . . what's that loud vacuuming sound I hear? Why it's Twitter sucking all your time away! This is a reality you're going to face all too soon. Twitter can take a ton of time, and it can also be fun and addictive. So let's tackle the issue head on by providing a few actionable ideas to keep this thing under control.

11

Twitter Time-Savers

"How much time should I spend on Twitter?" is a question I get asked repeatedly.

There's no absolute answer to that question, just like there is no good answer to how much money a company should spend on advertising or how many resources should be devoted to research and development. It is completely dependent on your goals and the competitive structure of your business.

The time needed to do social media marketing right is a significant obstacle for many organizations. Part of the reason for this is that the duties are frequently piled on top of already-full plates at work. That's not fair, it's not smart, and it's not going to work as a long-term strategy.

Instead I'd like to have you rethink your entire approach to marketing and how new social media channels like Twitter fit in. Your customers are probably spending more time on social networking sites and less time on ads, trade shows, and journals. Even views of most traditional websites are down in the past few years. Maybe it's time to rethink how you split up your entire budget and the time you're spending with traditional media and other networking channels.

When I started my own business many years ago, I devoted an enormous amount of time and expense to live networking meetings. You know the type. Chamber of commerce meetings. Networking "speed dating." Trade shows. Business Networking International.

At the time I started my business, this seemed to be the only alternative. My last "corporate job" was global in nature. For years I had been leading teams in China, Russia, Brazil, Australia—almost every corner of the world—and really had no significant business connections in my own region of the country! So I had to get out and press the flesh.

I dutifully began the circuit of lunch and breakfast meetings, hoping beyond hope that a conversation would lead to a connection and connections would turn into customers. It was an endless loop of meeting the same insurance salespeople, bug exterminators, and realtors over and over again.

Then came the moment that made me realize I *had* to find another way. I attended a local networking meeting called "TNT." I can't remember what it stood for, but I'm pretty sure the middle word was "Networking"! At the beginning of the meeting, people stood up and said something nice about their business. At the end of each uplifting description, the whole room yelled "Boom!" TNT— get it? I didn't know it was coming, and after that first boom, somebody had to peel me off the ceiling.

This just wasn't for me. And it wasn't working anyway. Sure, I met lots of nice people, but they were all trying to sell something to *me*, too. I acquired a few small local customers, but they were unprepared to think and work on the strategic level I enjoyed. They needed yard signs, not company strategies. If I stuck with it, I could have made a living, but I needed to paint on a much bigger canvas.

And these meetings were taking up too much valuable *time*. Some of the events were lasting an hour and half or more every week, plus travel time. When I discovered Twitter, I realized that I could connect with highly targeted individuals instead of taking potluck each week. And I could cast my net more broadly—globally, in fact—without ever leaving my office. I could connect on my time, my terms, and my schedule. In my pajamas.

As the enormous benefits of Twitter networking accumulated, I stopped going to the time-consuming and expensive local meetings completely. Today I have a thriving international business built almost entirely through social networking. My four largest customers, my five most important collaborators, and my teaching position at Rutgers University all came to me via Twitter connections.

Now don't misunderstand. I'm not saying there is no value to live networking. Of course, there are powerful benefits for many people, and there always will be. I'm only saying that for *my individual strategy*, online networking became a more effective source for qualified leads and business value. My point is, I could spend more than an hour a day on Twitter, and it would still save valuable time compared with what I was doing before. It's something to think about.

So how much time does it take? If you're just starting out, let me suggest you put a stake in the ground and devote at least 20 minutes a day. I am not saying *limit* your time to 20 minutes—chances are, you will want to spend more time than that! But if you want to get going and you are time stressed, I'm going to provide a manageable plan to keep you moving in the right direction.

Actually, I am going to provide you with three plans for how you should spend 20 minutes a day: one is for beginners, one is for intermediate users, and the third is for the more experienced Twitterati.

The 20-Minute Regimen for Beginners

In a world obsessed with "engagement" and "conversation," I'm going to offer some unconventional advice—forget about it for a few weeks. If you're a beginner and can only spend 20 minutes a day on Twitter, concentrate on Tao Lesson Number One: building a relevant tribe of followers, for the reasons we've already covered.

So in the first two months, tweet at least once a day so people see that you're active, but spend most of your time finding and following interesting people using the many techniques discussed in Chapter 5. Don't worry if people follow back or not. That will come in time. Building an engaged, meaningful tribe is the prerequisite to any future success.

Now for the other half of your time, spend it reading, and occasionally responding to, tweets from your new friends. This will give you the chance to see what kind of tweets you like, which is instructive when you start tweeting more heavily yourself. This will also begin to get you in the rhythm of Twitter and on your way to creating fascinating new relationships.

Continue with this regimen until you have 200 relevant followers.

Intermediate Tweeting in 20 Minutes a Day

Let's consider the intermediate phase to occur when you have around 200 followers. This is an arbitrary number of course, but it gives you a goal to shoot for.

Once you have the momentum of 200 followers, relevant people will begin to organically follow you, so the emphasis should now be on sharing, connecting, and adding value to your new tribe.

Get into the habit of tweeting content as you're reading throughout the day. Simply hit that **Tweet** button that is now associated with nearly every piece of content on the web. This takes no time at all. You might want to add a short comment like "Valuable" or "Made me laugh" at the front of the retweet to stir more sharing and engagement.

With more than 200 followers, Twitter is probably starting to get a little noisy, so it's time to take two new actions to help you spend your time more efficiently.

First, create your first Twitter Lists, which categorize your followers and make tweet reading so much more efficient. Scan through some of your new Lists once or twice a day and look for opportunities to thank people, retweet individuals, answer a question, or offer help. This might be a good time to reread Chapter 10.

Second, sign up for a third-party Twitter interface like TweetDeck or Hootsuite. Import your new Lists into these apps to make it easy to look across your tribes for news and interesting tweets. These platforms offer a lot of features that will be covered in Chapter 13. I also recommend that you download your platform of choice onto your mobile device (free) so you can use the idle time you're spending in line at the bank or during a TV commercial break to catch up with your Twitter friends.

In this intermediate phase, I would encourage you to concentrate your 20 minutes a day primarily on the content-sharing skills I introduced in Chapter 6. Now it's time to earn your keep with this new audience. Engage a few minutes every day to earn those connections—and create those conversations—that can deliver business benefits.

If you are working for a business and trying to build a brand on Twitter, begin salting in interesting and relevant pieces of your company's "rich content"—blog posts, videos, and other assets that can help you build your voice of authority. There might even be ways to help people in your Twitter audience with links to your company content.

The 20-Minute Challenge for Twitter Pros

Congratulations. If you have more than 400 followers on Twitter, you are in the top 10 percent of all Twitter users!

At this point in your Twitter journey, you should be getting comfortable with the rhythm and language of

Twitter. And let's face it: if you're really immersed in Twitter, the challenge is probably how not to spend *all* your time on this addictive little channel! Once you have surrounded yourself with interesting people, it's easy to "go down the rabbit hole" and follow link after fascinating link.

Now that you have exceeded 400 followers, you should be good at managing your Lists, mastering a platform like Hootsuite (including mobile), and building a few good friendships among your new favorite tweeters.

Again following the premise that you only have 20 minutes a day, the focus at this point should be on the third aspect of Tao: Authentic Helpfulness. Yes, you still need to build your audience—this never ends if you are doing this for business purposes—and, yes, the focus must always be on sharing great commentary and content, but to take this to the next level and really activate this channel, you need to engage, using some of the ideas from Chapter 7.

Here are some ideas to place the focus on others and build a reputation as a valued Twitter resource:

- Continue to build up your Twitter Lists and look for opportunities to help and engage each day. Sharing other people's content is a great way to get on their radar screen.
- If you are in business and are looking to speed up the rate of your audience building, consider Twitter

advertising options. These options can more or less automate some of the audience-building activities, but it takes virtually no time at all after the initial setup. This may not be cost effective for smaller businesses, but I encourage you to experiment and see if it brings value to your marketing efforts. I'll cover the options in Chapter 16.

- Try engaging at different times of the day to reach different people in your audience. For example, I am generally most active on Twitter before my workday begins and maybe in the late afternoon. If you are only sending out tweets in the late morning, I may never connect with you. A handy tool like Buffer can help you fan out your tweets throughout the day.

- Start looking at some of the more advanced options on platforms like Hootsuite and TweetDeck. For example, you can easily post the same content to multiple accounts, sort your followers by different criteria, and receive analytics reports so you can track which tweets are doing the best with your audience.

- Don't get caught in a "List bubble." Every once in a while, look at your general Twitter stream and see if there is anybody who catches your attention. People change; jobs change; priorities change. Always keep an eye on building and renewing your Lists.

Outsourcing: The Ultimate Time-Saver?

Can you outsource your tweeting to an advertising or PR agency? Perhaps that would be the ultimate time-saving measure?

You should always strive to be genuine on Twitter, as with all other marketing activity, and if you are creating a personal profile attached to an individual, then that individual should always do his or her own tweets. Period.

I have a friend who had been building a Twitter relationship with a business executive she admired. They had tweeted back and forth a few times, and he had provided some helpful career advice to her. When they had a chance to finally meet at a networking event, she introduced herself and was met with a puzzled stare. He had never heard of her before and sheepishly explained that his PR agency was tweeting for him. Obviously his reputation was ruined for this young woman . . . and also to all those she talked to about the incident!

In a well-publicized snafu, a PR agency rep tweeting on behalf of Chrysler Corporation sent out this tweet: "I find it ironic that Detroit is known as the #motorcity when no one here knows how to f**cking drive."

He thought he was tweeting from his personal account, but in fact, it came from Chrysler's Twitter account by mistake. He lost his job, and the agency lost the account.

Faking it on Twitter is dangerous business.

But you may be in a situation where you have no other practical choice than to "team-tweet" behind a brand name; then you could outsource or share the tweeting among a few trusted individuals. If you do outsource:

- Be clear and realistic on your objectives.
- Have clear lines of who owns what.
- Have a clear plan for content, tone, and frequency.
- Be prepared to take advice and listen to it. Most experts know what they are doing, and it's in their best interests to make it work for you.

Make sure that you have a disaster recovery plan in case of a PR upset. If you're using an agency, ask the people there to show you how they are managing your account distinctly from personal accounts and from other client accounts, so that tweets aren't mistakenly sent via the wrong account—easy to do when you're using a sharing platform. Ask to meet everyone who will be tweeting via your account and create some rules or guidelines for tweeting.

Outsourcing doesn't mean abdicating responsibility— make sure you are involved and holding everyone to account.

Before you outsource, carefully weigh the risks and benefits. One of the biggest opportunities of social media is "humanizing" the brand, and even the biggest brands are finding ways to do that successfully. In the long term, businesses should aim at involving their own employees to be "brand beacons" on Twitter instead of relying on an outside agency.

12

Balancing Personal and Professional

What is the proper balance between personal and professional outreach on Twitter? If you are using an account to promote company and client content, is it also appropriate to carry on conversations on a personal level about sports, a great recipe, or your favorite charity? Do you need to have *two accounts?*

This is a great question and one that I have to address on two levels, philosophical and practical.

As you have probably realized by now, there are many different uses for Twitter, but when it comes to business, I think, at its heart, Twitter is a powerful networking tool . . . which is what many companies and individuals don't understand. They view the platform as just another way to broadcast company advertising and press releases. By trying to force-fit old "broadcast" media thinking into this new platform, they are suboptimizing Twitter at best and hurting their brand at worst.

Think of yourself in another networking situation . . . say, an industry conference or a chamber of commerce meeting. Would you stand there and read press releases? No, of course not. You would seek out great people to connect with, discuss subjects that are interesting to them, and eventually look for ways to work together. Twitter can work exactly the same way.

So even if you are playing a business role on Twitter, there is no reason you can't be yourself, unless you are a naturally mean and sucky person. If you are in that category, you have to either not be mean and sucky or not use Twitter. And if you are truly, chronically mean and sucky, you probably will fail at business anyway, let alone Twitter, so it's better that you find out sooner than later, I suppose.

When networking, the most powerful relationships are built on trust and friendship, so it's OK to let people know a little bit more about what is going on in your life, including your love of sports, charity, and family. As you go throughout your day, just tweet what is interesting to you, as long as it is appropriate and professional.

In most cases, I do not think it makes sense to have both a personal and business account. You're not two people, and being yourself is not only a great way to build your business network; it humanizes your company brand.

OK, now I'll get off my soapbox and examine some practical realities. Even if you have this concept down, maybe your company doesn't. If your job is to be your official company Twitterer, you probably have marching orders to follow a role or social media policy that has you tweeting behind a logo. You might even have a (gasp) script. Here's what you should do in that case: follow the company policy. Don't lose your job over Twitter. You can still work to change attitudes over time. Buy your boss a copy of *The Tao of Twitter*. We'll both thank you.

The Five Types of Twitter Accounts

There are several compromises or hybrid strategies for blending personal and professional approaches on Twitter. Here are the five types of organizational Twitter accounts. Which one fits for you?

1. All Business All the Time

In some cases it is entirely appropriate to "broadcast" over Twitter. Here's an example: Citi has a site (@CitiJobTweets) that only broadcasts job openings. The company really doesn't need to engage in a conversation, and it's not even trying. The account follows nobody. It lists jobs, people want them, . . . and they subscribe to the account. It's that simple. Citi could probably work to build a community, but why? This is simply a broadcast channel.

2. Tweeting Under Cover

Many of the world's most important brands have teams
of tweeters engaging with the public behind a corporate
logo. A common practice is to tweet with the initials of
the tweeter at the end of each tweet and to have someplace
to learn about who is actually behind the tweets—a link
on the Twitter profile page is a common way to provide
this information; so is a list of names and initials on the
Twitter background. I like this best practice because
it allows real human connection even in a big corporate
environment. A tweet might look like this: "Glad to
help you @username. Thank you for using our
product!—MWS."

This is a low-effort, low-risk option to humanize the
brand and still operate under one brand banner that is
commonplace today.

3. Blending Personal and Corporate

In some cases corporate accounts are assigned to
individuals, especially in customer service roles.

So for example, you might have an account called
@ATTSusan or @CiscoJeff (I made those up). This account
would feature a real person and a real photo, but the account
is owned by the company. When that person moves on, the
profile would change to a new name and a new person in
that role in the company.

4. Real Persons in Real Time

Usually the best option is to have real people representing your company, like my friend Chad Parizman (@cparizman), who works for HGTV. His profile states "#SocialTV for HGTV & DIY Network. Yankee Fan. Web Analytics Geek."

The ultimate goal for many companies is to get to a place where a number of employees can serve as beacons for your brand. Chad clearly identifies himself as an HGTV employee but is free to build his own connections through his own personality and content. Of course, he also knows that in some respect he is always "on" for HGTV.

Creating these employee "beacons" for a brand is a key idea. Over a period of years, I became friends with a fellow in London who worked in IT for a huge global consulting firm. When he learned that I was coming to the United Kingdom on a business trip, he introduced me to his company's marketing leadership, and I ended up conducting a very successful social media workshop for the company.

I didn't get connected to this company through the normal channels. In fact, the whole event was planned without a phone call. To me, my IT friend *was the face of this company*, and it resulted in concrete business benefits for his firm. Wouldn't it be amazing to unleash the power of every person in your organization as a potential salesperson?

5. Fake and Fun

A recent trend is creating entertaining Twitter accounts based on fake characters. Coke has created a hilarious account based on the quips from the company's long-dead founder (@docpemberton). A restaurant in Seattle has an account for its french fries, Geico Insurance unleashes its witty gecko mascot on Twitter, and even the iconic Mr. Clean flexes his Twitter muscles for his brand of cleaning products.

PART 2
Advanced Concepts

13

Next Steps

Believe it or not, your Twitter journey is just beginning.
This chapter contains a few advanced ideas to help you get
even more benefits from the platform. If you're a beginner,
it might be a good idea to take a month, or even two, to
master the basic concepts of the Tao before jumping into
these ideas. But if you have a handle on it, here are some
interesting new things to explore.

Activity Stream

If you click the **Discover** button at the top of the navigation
bar, you'll see a prompt for **Activity**. This is a timeline of *all*
the Twitter-related activities for *all* your followers. This is
interesting (and perhaps a little overwhelming!) and can be
a great source to find new lists and followers.

Alerts

If electrical services go down, often the only way people can stay informed during a crisis is through their mobile devices. Twitter began a program to insert emergency alert notifications into user Twitter streams. By enrolling in Twitter Alerts, an organization can push an alert through Twitter during an emergency or natural disaster or whenever other communication services aren't accessible. You typically have to go to an emergency response organization's website or Twitter profile page to subscribe to the emergency alert push notification system.

Analytics

At some point in your journey, you are probably going to want some analytics to help you look for Twitter trends and successes, especially if you are doing this for a business. The good news is, there are many wonderful software applications available to fit any budget—from enterprise level to an individual entrepreneur. The bad news is that this segment is in constant churn—new applications, mergers, changes in business direction—so that any recommended list would be obsolete by the time you read this.

There is a little trick you can try to get some meaningful feedback on your Twitter presence. You can actually tap into the analytics capabilities of the Twitter advertising site without ever taking out an ad! Here's how:

1. Go to https://ads.twitter.com/.
2. Sign in with your Twitter account information.
3. At the top of the navigation bar, click **Activity.**
4. Then select **Tweets.**

This will deliver a dashboard with a report of your recent follow-unfollow activity, the performance of your tweets, and an ability to sort and download a simple report. The biggest limitations of this application are that it only reports the last 30 days' activities and that it doesn't allow for any insights into who is most actively engaging with you. If you need something more than this simple report, my recommendation is to do a web search for "Twitter analytics" and look for a recent blog post comparing the prices and capabilities of available services.

Audience Maintenance

When your tribe grows beyond a few hundred people, you will probably want to clean out some of the folks who have never followed you back or those who have become inactive. There are lots of applications to help you do this, but it's also a rapidly changing scene. My recommendation is to do a Google search or even a Twitter search for "Twitter maintenance applications" and find suggestions on the best available applications. There are both paid and free options.

If you are just starting out, don't worry about audience maintenance as a priority, but once you get above 200 followers, you might look at this once a month.

Brand Pages

Twitter's brand pages utility offers several features for businesses, including the most prominently Promoted Tweets and an enhanced design. Brands can "pin" a Promoted Tweet to the top of their timeline, making it the first thing a visitor is likely to see. Companies can use this space to promote videos, images, links, and more.

Custom Timelines

Twitter allows you to develop your own Twitter stream that could be useful if you want to show a stream of tweets at a conference or customer event, for example. If you want to highlight just a few tweeters, customers, celebrities, attendees, etc., this can be a useful application. Custom timelines can be created within TweetDeck, which is owned by Twitter.

Geolocation or Geotagging

The use of location data in Tweets adds a pin to your post to tell people where you are in real time. This is an option in your settings and can be used by certain applications to identify Twitter followers near you. Most people are not using this option. Think through the safety implications of broadcasting your location before changing this setting.

Lead Generation Cards

If you advertise through Twitter, you can add a "business card" to your tweet that allows you to collect contact information from a potential client and integrate it into a CRM system. More on this in Chapter 16.

Legal Implications

Publishing on Twitter creates a permanent and searchable record of your statements. While it's important to be real, it's also important to be careful. My favorite local pizza proprietor was sued for $2 million after posting an unflattering tweet about his advertising agency. Even after he deleted the tweet, his adversary had kept an image of the tweet and pursued the lawsuit. Tweets are tiny but carry the same legal weight as a blog post or news article.

In a corporate environment, lawyers should be involved in determining the social media policy to account for laws and regulations specific to your industry.

I'm not suggesting that you become paranoid, but just be aware that you're always publishing. The news is filled with stories about companies and individuals who have been embarrassed by inappropriate tweets that go viral. Even if you delete a tweet, if somebody else has retweeted it, that content still exists out there.

Listening Platforms

Once you get above about 200 followers or so, it becomes increasingly difficult to follow the conversations. You'll be facing a daily wall of noise! At this point you need to bring in help by downloading a free or low-cost "listening" platform to organize your conversations.

There are many, many options in this area, but two of the most popular are Hootsuite and TweetDeck (which is owned by Twitter). I've already mentioned these tools as a way to schedule tweets, save searches, and save time.

The primary advantage of these applications is the ability to organize followers into logical groups according to your Twitter Lists. For example, you might create a List called "Industry Experts" and another called "Local

Friends." That way you can isolate and segment the people you *really* want to listen to and follow their conversations.

These apps also have the ability to save Twitter searches so that you can see a stream of targeted information of interest to you. There are many other little tricks and useful tools built into these apps to make it much easier and fun to follow along on Twitter. All have versions for smartphones and other mobile devices.

There are also advanced paid options with important utilities for managing your social media stream across an enterprise or small business.

Period Before @mention

This is the one mistake almost everyone makes on Twitter. If you start a tweet with "@username" without a period before the "@" symbol, only your mutual followers (in other words, people who follow both you and the person you are mentioning) and the person you're tweeting will see your tweet. If the person is mentioned within the tweet, all followers will see it. Here is a summary:

- A tweet from you that starts with "@markwschaefer" will only be seen by me, you, and the people who follow both of us.

- A tweet that starts ".@markwschaefer" will be seen by me, you, and everybody who follows us.
- If you mention me in the middle of a tweet, like "I read @markwschaefer's book The Tao of Twitter," it will also be visible to all our followers.

Second Screen

Twitter is sometimes referred to as the "second screen." When people watch television, they frequently engage with social media platforms at the same time. The engagement with this second screen can be an important amplification of the original programming and advertisements. Analyzing these interactions has become an important focus for Twitter and its monetization plans.

Social Media Policies

Many companies are encouraging employees to tweet, post, and blog on behalf of the business. But what are the "rules"? What constitutes abuse? How much time should employees spend on social media at work? What if employees access inappropriate sites?

All these questions should be addressed in a social media policy. Every organization should have a policy— even if employees can't access the social web via company computers, it's likely they are getting online through their smartphones. To be fair to everybody, employees need to know through an effective policy what's expected and what's at risk.

Here's a website with hundreds of examples of organizational social media policies: http://socialmediagovernance.com/policies.php.

Spam

Twitter began to gather steam as a popular social media platform in 2009 and became so overrun by hackers and spammers that the service was almost becoming unusable. The company has done a good job cleaning up its act, but the spammers are always coming up with new tricks.

"Spamming" can describe a variety of annoying or unethical online behaviors. Here are some common tactics used by spam accounts:

- Posting harmful links (including links to phishing or malware sites)
- Abusing the @reply or @mention function to post unwanted messages to users
- Spamming Trending Topics to try to grab attention
- Repeatedly posting duplicate updates

- Using aggressive following behavior (for instance, mass following and unfollowing in order to gain attention)

Another sign of a spam is when you get a direct message that contains only a link or a strange message such as "Aren't you embarrassed by this" with a link. This is a signal that the message sender's account has been hacked, so *please be very cautious* before clicking any suspicious link.

It would be difficult to provide complete guidelines on this subject because the tactics change so often. The problems are usually more in the category of annoying versus dangerous, but you should still actively report undesirable behavior for spam. This action doesn't immediately cause an account to be suspended, but it's an important tool Twitter uses to identify and investigate spam accounts.

Tailored Audience

Twitter's advertising program pushes your tweets as ads to targeted user accounts across the web.

Tailored Trends

As a default, Twitter adjusts the Trending Topics on the left column of your profile based on your location and interests.

If you look carefully, in the **Trend** box, there is a word that says **Change**. If you want to see the global Trending Topics, you can adjust that by clicking that word.

Twitter Blogs

Twitter is constantly changing and improving. To keep up with the latest ideas, I recommend following the official Twitter blog at http://blog.twitter.com/.

If you decide to become active on Twitter advertising initiatives, I also highly recommend that you pay attention to Twitter's advertising blog. The company makes frequent changes to its offerings that can impact your business. You can find that blog at https://blog.twitter.com/advertising.

Verified Accounts

On certain accounts (especially those of celebrities), you'll see a little blue check mark next to the user name. This means that account is verified to be the real person. It's so easy to set up fake accounts that this function has become necessary to protect some people who are in the public spotlight.

Not everybody can obtain a verified account. Twitter proactively verifies accounts on an ongoing basis, concentrating on highly sought users in music, acting, fashion, government, politics, religion, journalism, media, sports, and business.

From Twitter's website: "We do not accept requests for verification from the general public. If you fall under one of the above categories and your Twitter account meets our qualifications for verification, we may reach out to you in the future."

Vine

Vine is a popular application founded by Twitter that allows you to embed six-second videos into tweets and other social media content.

Website Cards

In 2014, Twitter began rolling out the Website Card, which is similar to the Lead Generation Card but allows users to easily discover interesting content while giving advertisers the ability to drive a higher volume of clicks.

You have to be a Twitter advertiser to enable this functionality, but it is useful, since relevant and targeted Twitter users (prequalified by interests and keywords) can preview an image, related context, and a call to action in their timelines before tapping on a link.

The card can also be used in conjunction with conversion tracking to measure the end-to-end conversion from a tweet engagement or an impression to an action in your sales funnel, such as a sign-up or purchase.

14

Becoming a Top Cat on Twitter Chats

There is one advanced concept that has exploded in
popularity and deserves a special section of its own:
Twitter chats.

The idea is very simple. A group of people with a
common interest gather together at a designated time to
share ideas and discussion. The discussion is united by a
hashtag so that all can follow along. For example, #CMChat
gathers people who are in the country music business,
and #CookingChat brings together cooking enthusiasts.
There are chats for every imaginable interest, and the list is
growing all the time.

There are several powerful benefits of chats:

- Chats are a great place to learn and exchange ideas
  with like-minded individuals from around the world.

- Chats are an excellent place to meet interesting
  new contacts. When you find a chat that you like, it
  would be a good idea to follow these individuals and
  perhaps even create a list of your favorite chat group
  members.
- Chats are a great place to gain awareness for your
  own brand and ideas.
- Participating in chats creates connections and
  content that can enhance your personal influence.
- A company, brand, or individual can establish a voice
  of authority by creating and leading a chat.
- Chats have become so popular, some companies are
  paying advertising fees to sponsor them. Yes, you
  can make money from hosting a Twitter chat!

So how do you get started?

The first thing to do is find a relevant chat that you will
enjoy. The best way to keep up with this dynamic list is to do
a web search for "Twitter chat schedule," and you'll find a
detailed list of chats by subject, day, and time. It will also list
the leaders of the chat and sometimes provide a link to the
most recent session.

Once you pick your chats, there are a couple of ways
to participate. First, follow the people who run these
chats and get their updates on upcoming sessions. When
the chat is scheduled to happen, you can search for the

designated hashtag in Twitter. The best way to follow along is to use a free service like TweetChat or TwitterFall, platforms specifically designed to enhance your Twitter chat experience.

A word of warning: On the most popular chats, the tweets may be coming at a furious rate! It can be challenging to follow along when there are concurrent conversations.

Participation is key for reaping the benefits of Twitter chats. Ask and answer questions, add insights, discuss. These are usually very open and friendly forums, so don't be worried about posting a "stupid" comment or question.

Many times, there are predetermined questions, and the moderator will pose these in the form of this example: "Q1 What is the best way to get value from a Twitter chat?" Participants answer accordingly: "A1 One idea is to participate actively and help newcomers."

Creating Your Own Chat

Hosting your own chat can be a fun and rewarding way to create community around your ideas and subject matter. Let's walk through the steps of creating a new Twitter chat.

Setup

First, you should secure a descriptive hashtag. At http://www.Twubs.com you can see if your hashtag has already been taken and reserve one for your chat. Once you have a unique name, it would be a good idea to reserve a Twitter handle for the chat, too.

To promote the chat, you may want to create a home base for your community on Facebook, a LinkedIn group, or a blog where you can make announcements and post completed conversations.

You'll also need to pick a time and regular date for the chat. Every Monday? The second Tuesday of the month? Find a date that fits your schedule, because as the moderator, you are creating a long-lasting commitment to your community. Some chat communities have co-moderators or even shared responsibility among all the members to spread the responsibility.

Planning the Chat

In preparation for your first chat, you'll want to personally invite a few friends to get the momentum going. Create enough topic questions ahead of time to propel at least 30 minutes of chat. Involve your community in choosing topics and questions. Other chats are just free-flowing with no assigned agenda. They're simply a place to meet and touch base.

Many chats feature special guests who help answer questions and engage with participants. So, for example, I have been a guest "speaker" on book chats, marketing chats, and leadership chats, to name a few. If you are asked to be a guest on a chat, be sure to have the questions prepared ahead of time so you can get ready with at least a few tweetable responses. It can be difficult to keep up with the frenzied pace of conversation through coherent 140-character responses!

Post-chat and Promotion

As the moderator, you are creating some very valuable, shareable content, so be sure to capture this. There are several free platforms to do this, including RowFeeder, ChirpStory, and Storify. You can post this content on your Facebook or blog and then promote the content to attract new members.

Promoting a link to your home base in industry publications, social media outlets, and related forums is another way to find people who might be interested in the topic.

Another best practice is to e-mail a transcript to your community members after the chat. This will serve as a reminder of the next chat and also keep people in the loop even if they miss the event.

During the chat, everyone participating will be tweeting with the hashtag in the tweet. Just the act of having the chat is a great way to promote the event. I'll often join in a chat when I see an interesting hashtag pop up from a friend.

As long as you stick to a consistent schedule and provide interesting content, your attendance will pick up over time.

Just like everything else, Twitter chats have limitations. The 140-character maximum can limit the depth of a commentary, and even good ideas can get lost in a big chat. The sheer volume of tweets does not create an environment for accurate sharing of information. Still, the serendipitous connections you make in these forums are often more important than the actual content of the chat.

15

The Awesome Power of Twitter Search

Many business professionals believe the Twitter search function is the most powerful tool for marketing insight ever created.

If you search Google, Bing, or Yahoo!, your results will be articles, videos, and websites. But if you search Twitter, the results are real-time conversations. And you can learn a lot from tapping into conversations!

Used effectively, Twitter search can be an essential tool for discovery and marketing research. And people are catching on—there are nearly 3 billion search queries performed on Twitter every day!

The basics of the search are extremely easy to master. You can insert any name, phrase, or hashtag in the search box at the top of the profile page and find some useful results.

An Indispensable Guide to Effective Search

To really unlock the power of content on Twitter, it's useful to know some advanced search operators. You can dramatically improve your search results by typing these directions directly into the search box.

Typing this:	Shows you tweets that:
lang:en	Are only in the English language
funny movies	Contain both "funny" and "movies." This is the default operator.
"Steelers win"	Contain the *exact phrase* "Steelers win"
man OR woman	Contain either "man" or "woman" (or both)
Steelers-football	Contain "Steelers" but not "football"
#Steelers	Contain the hashtag "#Steelers"
from:markwschaefer	Were sent from person "markwschaefer"
to:markwschaefer	Were sent to person "markwschaefer"
@markwschaefer	Referencing person "markwschaefer"
"Chinese restaurant" near:"chicago"	Contain the exact phrase "Chinese restaurant" and sent near Chicago
near:NYC within:15mi	Were sent within 15 miles of New York City
"Chinese restaurant" since:2013-07-30	Contain the phrase "Chinese restaurant" and sent since date "2013-07-30" (year-month-day)
"Steelers" -attend 😃	Contain the phrase "Steelers" but not "attend," with a positive sentiment
flight 🙁	Contain the word "flight," with a negative sentiment

Typing this:	Shows you tweets that:
Flight ?	Contain the word "flight," and tweet is asking a question
hilarious filter:links	Contain the word "hilarious" and linking to a URL

More Search Tips

Three more essential search tips to keep in mind include:

1. Keep your search as simple as possible. More complex searches miss more tweets.
2. There is often more than one variation of popular hashtags (for example, #FollowFriday and #FF mean the same thing).
3. Sometimes a search won't show you older tweets because there are too many results. Consider doing one or more searches using the **before:** and **since:** date operators.

It is also a good idea to save common searches to save time typing in this search every day. Twitter allows you to save searches, but I find it most helpful to turn to a third-party platform because you can save a search and it shows up as a constantly updating column of tweets in your stream. This can be a valuable source of leads, ideas, and insights as conversations unfold minute by minute.

There are limitless possibilities for the ways you can combine these advanced search operators to help your business. Think about using advanced search techniques to discover:

- People in your town who need your product or service
- Positive sentiment about restaurants, hotels, and entertainment venues in a new city you are visiting
- Relevant new contacts who are already expressing interest in your product
- Conversations expressing a negative sentiment about your competition
- People using your product in new ways
- People using phrases that might indicate political alignment, an interest in a cause, or expertise that can help you
- Influential online personalities mentioning your product

Search in Action

Here is just a small illustration of the potential. I just did a simple search for people in my hometown (population 600,000) talking about pizza. There is at least one mention of pizza every 20 minutes, on average, and the rate is higher during lunchtime and dinnertime. Remember, the beauty of Twitter is that tweets are public, so the search results are not just for the people you are following. These are results from every single person meeting your search criteria.

Here is a sample of local, pizza-related tweets in my city over a four-hour period. If you owned a pizza place in this town, what business benefits could you derive by discovering people publishing the following tweets?

- "Craving pizza but I'm broke. Where can I get pizza for some change in my pocket??"
- "I want a really unhealthy burger, but there's also Cici's macaroni pizza."
- "What Pizza Looks Like Around the World: Turkish pizza looks yummy!" *(included a link to a photo essay on pizza)*
- "I just dropped the pizza face front on the floor. I REALLY suck."
- "Not a good night for cooking. Thinking pizza."
- "My parents are coming for a visit. What's the best pizza parlor in town?"
- "I just got so excited making a Lean Cuisine pizza. I really worked my butt off in the kitchen! LOL"
- "Can you cook pizza in a toaster?"
- "Dear delivery pizza people: You are all pansies for not delivering pizza today. The roads are not that bad!"
- "The weather is bad but Papa John's is still delivering. Thank you Papa John's!!"

Together, we could probably brainstorm some interesting business tactics from following this stream of tweets on an hourly basis. Some of the business opportunities might include:

- Finding new customers. Discover people in your delivery area who love pizza. This is your ideal Twitter community, right? Follow those people and put them on a List!
- Developing "human" relationships. Tweet back to create human, personal relationships with people in your city who talk about pizza.
- Offering helpful advice. Provide helpful advice for people who have questions about buying pizza on a budget, cooking pizza in a toaster, or wanting a recommendation for a family dinner ("Stop by our restaurant and your beverages on are on us!").
- Doing competitor research. Who has delivery cars on the move? Who is failing?
- Contemplating new product development. Macaroni pizza? Turkish pizza? What makes Lean Cuisine so good? Should we offer a diet or healthy version?
- Creating buzz. One person in your town ruined her pizza by dropping it on the floor. What do you think would happen if you tweeted her back publicly to tell her you wanted to deliver a whole new pizza to her free of charge so she's not hungry?

- Serving as a content source. The link to pizza from around the world sounds interesting. If you have surrounded yourself with a local group of pizza fanatics, they might love to see a retweet from you on this!

You see from this little case study that even a small, family-owned pizza parlor could create transformational business benefits simply by paying attention to what people are saying on the Twitter stream. I hope you'll experiment with these advanced search options and find ways to grow your business!

16

Advertising on Twitter

Most of this book has been dedicated to creating business benefits by building organic connections on Twitter. But I would be remiss if I didn't also mention the paid opportunities to reach customers through this platform. In fact, there is probably no social media platform that has worked harder at providing new advertising models and analytics than Twitter. The platform has always had a lot of heart, but since the first edition of this book, Twitter has also added a lot of muscle!

Undoubtedly, Twitter's advertising model will continue to evolve, but there are three primary strategies that will persist. In this chapter, I'll provide an overview of the main advertising opportunities—Promoted Tweets, Promoted Accounts, and Promoted Trends—along with a case study for each about an organization that has used the strategy effectively.

To get started on any of these promotional ideas, you'll have to find the Twitter for Business website, which is not easily discovered if you are on your main Twitter account. The website is https://business.twitter.com/. For each of these three advertising options, the Twitter business site walks you through an easy menu-driven set of instructions to set your campaign. Once you launch, Twitter provides a comprehensive real-time dashboard to track your progress.

The cost of these programs can vary widely—from a few dollars a day for a Promoted Tweet to several hundred thousand dollars a day for a Promoted Trend.

Promoted Tweets

Promoted Tweets look like regular tweets in a timeline but with the added bonus of reaching both current and potential followers you target by demographic characteristics, keywords, geographic location, or device. In this option, you can choose specific tweets to promote, or you can have Twitter automatically promote relevant tweets that you post.

When you send out a normal tweet, the opportunity for somebody to see your message is limited by:

- Who is in your audience.
- Who is paying attention to your tweets.

- Who is active on Twitter in some time range when you actually sent out the tweet. For example, even if people are interested in you and your tweets, they may not ever see a message if they are logged out for a period of time.

Promoted Tweets give you an opportunity to break through some of those barriers . . . for a price, of course.

- You can reach users at the right moment and in the right context (are their keywords or locations relevant to what you have to say?).
- The reach of your message can extend to people who are currently *not* in your audience.
- You can get a short-term lift to promote an event, deal, product, contest, or service.

There is a very big difference between an ad on Twitter and other types of pay-per-click advertising you might be accustomed to. On Twitter, you pay anytime somebody *engages* with that tweet, which includes mentioning the tweet, retweeting, favoriting the tweet, clicking on a hashtag, or clicking on a link. So keep in mind that if your goal is to drive leads by getting people to click, you may be paying for engagement that never leads anybody to your website!

Because of the complexity of the engagement metric, you need to really study what you are getting for your money and work diligently to keep optimizing your tweets to drive the desired actions. For example, if more people are clicking on a photo or a hashtag in a Promoted Tweet (engagement you are paying for), then maybe you should remove the photo or hashtag if your goal is new click-throughs to your site.

Another thing to consider is that you only pay for the "first generation" of impressions. This means if somebody retweets a Promoted Tweet and this person's followers click on your link, this is "free" advertising for you. So you will be rewarded for creating a really great tweet! This is a unique and valuable characteristic of the Twitter ad model.

When you create a Promoted Tweet campaign, you set a daily or total spending limit plus a "bid" per tweet. My research across several businesses shows that in general the amount you bid is far lower than what you actually pay. For example, I recently "bid" $1.50 per engagement on a tweet, and the actual cost was $0.19 per engagement.

Probably the biggest advantage to Twitter Promoted Tweets is that you can target people based on exactly what they are saying. In one example, a company that created a campaign to increase awareness about energy tariffs could use keyword targeting to find people complaining about tariffs. Once they complain, one of the next things they will see in their timeline is a Promoted Tweet from this company. A clever marketer could tailor a company's ads to align with

Trending Topics and news events related to the company's products and services.

Another example of an organization effectively using Promoted Tweets to reach a targeted audience in a time-sensitive situation is the American Red Cross (@RedCross), a nonprofit that helps communities to cope with disasters. What I love about this example is that the Red Cross actually had a sponsor for its Promoted Tweets. So in addition to being a very effective promotional campaign, it doubled as an indirect promotion (and tax write-off) for the campaign's sponsor, Craig Newmark, the founder of Craig's List.

Most individual and corporate giving occurs during the holiday season, but the competition for those dollars is fierce (especially in an economic downturn!).

During the Christmas season, the Red Cross launched a Promoted Tweets campaign to drive a matching-gift fund drive. A key to the campaign's success was spurring engagement by asking a fun and simple question: "What is your idea of the perfect gift?" The tweet included the hashtag #PerfectGift to organize the conversation and a link to the donation website. Newmark agreed to match each retweet or @reply with a $1 donation, up to $10,000.

The campaign drove an additional 2,400 mentions per day for the Red Cross, and the organization easily met its fund-raising target. But an unexpected benefit was an increased level of volunteer sign-ups and digital advocates for the charity who spent their time promoting the campaign on their own Twitter accounts.

Here are a few best practices to keep in mind as you consider this as an advertising option:

- Get really specific with your calls to action, and focus on the one key thing you want people to do. Strip away all distractions such as hashtags in your tweet that might lead to engagement you don't want to pay for.
- Don't be scared off by Twitter's estimated bid for Promoted Tweets. Experiment for a day to see the actual cost before refining your budget. Generally the actual cost is a fraction of the estimate.
- Continually experiment with the many targeting options Twitter provides. Look for ways to take advantage of shifts in real-time conversations among people who might be interested in your product.
- Take advantage of the deep analytics tools on Twitter and drill down into what's working and what's not. You can save a lot of money by paying attention to the feedback Twitter is providing you.
- In Chapter 13 I mentioned the idea of the Lead Generation Card. This is an interesting Twitter innovation that allows you to make a business offer and collect consumer contact information right from a

sponsored tweet. These information fields can then be integrated into your existing CRM system. If you want to learn more about this advertising option, there is plenty of information available on the Twitter business site at http://bit.ly/1gDKS2Z. This is what a Lead Generation Card might look like to your customers:

- Be aware that you are paying for engagement, so set your goals carefully. You are paying the same for a retweet, a mention, and a click, but they won't all be worth the same to your campaign.

Promoted Accounts

Twitter can help you boost your follower growth quickly through a program called Promoted Accounts. As I discussed previously, if you are trying to drive business benefits on Twitter, numbers do matter, as long as they are relevant, real people who have some possibility of engaging with you. The more people who are connecting with you, the more opportunities to ignite a spark of opportunity.

We already looked at Twitter's follower recommendations as a way to find people with whom you might connect. By purchasing a Promoted Account option, you are placing yourself at the top of that suggestion box to help people discover you. When you buy a Promoted Account option, it will make your account appear in five different places:

1. As part of the **Who to Follow** widget on the left side of home page
2. On the expanded **Who to Follow** Twitter page
3. People search results
4. On profile pages as part of the **Similar to you** widget
5. In the mobile home timeline on Twitter for iOS and Twitter for Android

When your account appears in one of these areas, it will be labeled as "Promoted."

Twitter's algorithms will try to show your account to people who might have some interest in you based on guidelines you set and also what might be relevant based on the demographics of their public Lists. For example, if you are a personnel recruiter looking to connect with civil engineers, Twitter may promote your account to people who have many civil engineers on their Lists.

Here is an example of how a small business used this effectively. Hampton Coffee (@HamptonCoffee) is a family-owned and community-focused espresso bar, café, and coffee roaster in the Hamptons, New York. The owners felt they had exhausted their ability to tap their local connections on Twitter, so they tried Promoted Accounts. Because they were able to target adults in a small geographic area relevant to their business, this option made sense for them.

In just a few weeks they had doubled the number of Twitter followers for the account. But a key to success was that the business owners also engaged with these new followers so they could build those high-potential business relationships.

Promoted Trends

Do you have a lot of money, and are you looking for massive exposure? Then Promoted Trends might be for you.

As we've already covered in Part 1, "Immersion," Trending Topics is a very popular feature that highlights the most popular conversations in the world. It might be gossip about a pop star, a sporting event like the Super Bowl, or a breaking news event. Clicking on a Trending Topic opens a world of conversation and even firsthand accounts of the latest news.

What if you could amplify your company's message, launch a product, or build awareness for an event you are sponsoring by placing your name at the very top of the list for an entire day? That's the idea behind Promoted Trends. When users click on your Promoted Trend, it takes them to your marketing message displayed through your Promoted Tweet.

There are fewer "targeting" options on this advertising opportunity—you can only choose by country. And bring plenty of money. It might cost you several hundred thousand dollars to be at the top of the charts for a day!

Most case studies for this opportunity involve megabrands because of the cost of the advertising platform. For example, EA Sports (@EASports) used a Promoted Trend to build excitement for the launch of a new soccer (or "football" in most parts of the world) FIFA-themed gaming product.

For the highly anticipated game launch, EA Sports wanted to align its brand with the beginning of the soccer season and latch on to the real-time conversations about FIFA. So the company was capitalizing on excitement that was already building among sports fans.

First, the company employed Promoted Tweets and targeted its core gaming audience and other relevant segments. The brand looked for Twitter users like those who follow major FIFA teams and sports news sources as well as those similar to @EASPORTSFIFA followers. It also targeted users who searched for terms related to FIFA games, players, and popular soccer-related hashtags.

As excitement built for the new season and the new game, the company finally launched its Promoted Trend associated with the hashtag #FIFA13 to massively amplify the promotion.

The Promoted Trend generated 38 percent engagement and drove more than 16 million impressions. Promoted Tweets in searches achieved a 15 percent engagement, and Promoted Tweets in timelines achieved a remarkable 17 percent engagement level.

On the day it launched its Promoted Trend, EA Sports received more than 10,000 mentions, three times the company's daily average.

Tailored Audiences

With tailored audiences, it's now possible to target Twitter users based on their actions across the web. Using a technique called cookie mapping, ad partners anonymously transfer a segment of users to Twitter (no personally identifiable information is exchanged). Once the transfer occurs, your segmented audience will be available in the

Twitter targeting system, and you're free to use it in your Twitter campaigns.

One of the nice things about tailored audiences is that you don't have to reinvent the wheel if you don't want to. Targeting Twitter users who have already visited your site— that is, using site retargeting—works great. While some users will tune out retargeted display banners, especially when they run too often, retargeted tweets are something novel and would probably grab a site visitor's attention. You can add personal touches and communicate the brand voice in a way that's just not possible with banner advertising.

The tailored audiences program is managed through a select group of Twitter-approved vendors. And some of those vendors come to the table with extremely valuable data on the terms people search on Google, Yahoo!, and Bing. That means that you can send targeted tweets to individuals who have searched for terms that are directly related to your brand. That's powerful because you can acquire entirely new customers—using the same technology that makes search engine marketing so effective.

Celebrity Endorsements

There is another "unofficial" way to pay for massive reach. Several third-party companies have lined up celebrities to endorse products through tweets. Some of these initiatives may run more than $250,000 per tweet.

There are legal nuances associated with these sponsored tweets since the Federal Trade Commission treats a tweet the same way as a published article or a blog post. If it is a paid endorsement, it must clearly state it is an ad, something that may be difficult to pull off in 140 characters!

17

25 Ideas to Toast Your Competition

Let's start putting some of these ideas to practical use for your business or organization. In fact, Twitter can be a powerful competitive advantage for many people!

Just because we're talking about marketing and competition, don't think I'm going to let you forget the "social" part of social media. Whether you work at a small business, a giant corporation, or a nonprofit, I'd like you to take a Post-it note, write "Social Media Is P2P" on it, and put this on your computer!

Social Media Is P2P

Person to person. This is the heart of our Tao, isn't it? If you take away one thing from this book—and it is the one thing most businesses disregard—remember that you are connecting to real people, not avatars. Somehow when we created this digital distance between ourselves and our customers, we forgot that there are real people out there! Business is built on relationships, and you are only working toward that end if you keep "P2P," not "press release," at the top of your mind.

There are lots of success stories and case studies documenting business success through Twitter. Here are a few of my favorite ways to leverage this platform for new business benefits.

1. Listen up! Twitter is a source of hugely valuable information for businesses. Its public nature and real-time status allow business users to research topics, follow market conditions, locate and learn about clients and their employees, follow relevant news, and much more. The scope for businesses using Twitter is enormous, from insurance companies being able to understand the day-to-day lifestyle of prospective life insurance candidates, to employers tracking which recruitment candidates are most suitable for their company, to even account managers using client timelines as a source of information they can use to enhance relationships.

Twitter as a tool for listening is frequently the first port of call for businesses choosing to embrace Twitter. Listening doesn't require action or even a Twitter account, which makes it a relatively safe approach to the platform.

Here is a powerful example of how this works. Bill Reighard (@BillReighard) is the founder of Food Donation Connection, a company that "rescues" surplus food from restaurants and other retailers at the end of the business day and delivers it to food banks to feed the hungry. He used well-managed Twitter Lists to watch potential clients for opportunities for engagement and connection.

Bill had been observing the online interactions that an executive from a large grocery chain was having with customers and activists. "Why don't you donate your surplus food?" the customer tweets were asking him. "Why are you throwing this good food away?"

After watching this exchange develop, Bill contacted the executive and said, "We can help you!" In less than a month, his company helped the grocery chain roll out a food donation program. It might not have happened without Twitter.

2. Enhance customer service. What's the world's favorite Twitter activity? Complaining! Which is

fine . . . unless the complaint is about you or your company! By digging deeper into Twitter, listening can mean far more than monitoring the frequency with which a keyword is used, instead giving businesses the ability to augment their customer support offerings from a relatively low-cost tool. Nearly every major business runs a significant part of both its B2B and B2C customer service function through social media, with Twitter taking a central focus. Advanced tools can also immediately rate the sentiment of complaints and the relative online influence of the person complaining.

3. Gather business intelligence. Twitter can be an incredibly powerful way to conduct business intelligence:

    - Follow your competitors' primary Twitter streams.
    - Monitor their replies (save a **search for** on Twitter).
    - Analyze their followers.
    - Monitor their score on Klout.com as a measure of their social media effectiveness.
    - Follow the Twitter streams of your competitors' employees.

4. Discover problems. Both human and automated monitoring systems are getting increasingly

sophisticated. Nissan of North America reported that its social media monitoring activities can pick up consumer trends four to six weeks faster than through traditional consumer feedback systems.

Consumer problems, product issues, and potentially damaging PR issues can be detected and even averted by picking up conversations about your company and responding quickly.

5. Break through communication barriers with tweets. Having a hard time making that business connection with a new lead through cold calls and e-mail? Try a tweet or direct message. The company may not return your calls, but it almost always returns tweets! I don't know the psychology behind this. I only know it works!

6. Run special deals and promotions. Create special deals and promotions on Twitter that you can use to drive traffic or move slow-moving stock. If you've done a good job surrounding yourself with Targeted Connections, they should be interested in your specials, right? A local bakery is using this idea to move its products quickly if it has baked too much of a certain item that day: "Come by before 4 p.m. for 2-for-1 coffee cakes." Hey, coffee cakes would certainly be meaningful content in my estimation! Especially cinnamon.

7. Build your brand. Twitter is an exceptional way to build your personal brand beyond your normal business borders. Even if you travel constantly, the opportunity for global reach through Twitter probably has more potential . . . with a lot less wear and tear.

8. Find new business contacts. You can do this through directories such as Twellow and the advanced Twitter search. Earlier in the book we discussed the concept of "prepopulating" new business relationships as a powerful networking advantage.

9. Take advantage of SEO. Did you know Twitter can help your visibility on search engines such as Google? Just a few years ago, search results would only turn up websites. Now you're just as likely to get LinkedIn profiles, video, and, yes, Twitter profiles and even individual tweets.

10. Use your tweets as real-time testimonies. Tweets are published and permanent, so feel free to use them as marketing tools. *An example:* One college featured real tweets about its school on an electronic highway billboard (not real time, of course!). A coffee shop featured happy customer tweets on a flat-screen display in its shop.

11. Use your tweets as public validation. As people send nice tweets about you, save them in your **favorite** Twitter function. When you need to pull out some "social validation," simply direct people to your Twitter page. This is public information for all to see.

12. Bear in mind that your tweets represent PR opportunities. Journalists are extremely active on Twitter, seeking information on story leads and sources. You might get some unexpected PR placements if you establish yourself as a voice of authority on Twitter, especially if you combine this with blogging.

13. Convert to real connections. I love the way businesses are using tweetups—networking meetings of Twitter enthusiasts—to effectively promote their organizations. Twitter loyalists love to get together to meet in real life—especially if free food is involved! If you have an appropriate meeting space or venue, why not sponsor a tweetup to introduce folks to your facility while giving them a friendly place to meet? I think this would be effective for restaurants and clubs, banks, nonprofits, schools, health clubs, real estate offices—almost any place with a large meeting space that serves local clients.

14. Stay abreast of trends. Twitter is a great way to keep up on the latest news and trends—what if you turned this into a competitive weapon for your entire organization? What would be the implications if your employees had access to real-time news and market information that your competitors don't have?

15. Own a chat. We've already covered Twitter chats in depth. But if your industry does not already have one, creating your own public chat can provide some competitive advantage as you connect to people interested in your chat topics. It is even possible to monetize chats.

16. Establish authority. Twitter is an excellent way to establish thought leadership for your brand in your community, especially if respected company executives are active on the site. The aim is to establish a leadership position in a particular field by creating and sharing content around a particular topic, as well as passing on opinions or statements on curated content. Many senior executives practice this approach using a personal account on behalf of a company.

17. Direct traffic. Through Twitter, offer helpful links and headlines that can drive traffic to your website, blog, landing pages, YouTube channels, Facebook, etc.

Despite the social media hype, your website is usually the place where you actually ask for money ... or registrations, downloads, uploads, or whatever you're after. Websites are still important in the social information ecosystem.

18. Connect through a funny persona. A few companies have successfully created funny and entertaining anonymous personas behind their brands. A taco restaurant in the Pacific Northwest makes wisecracks about its Mexi-fries. The fashion brand DKNY had an anonymous tweeter for years providing humorous insights into shopping experiences and the fashion world. Creating interest through funny alter-egos is risky business, but if you have the right personality, it can work.

19. Try Twitter advertising. If your competitor isn't doing any advertising on Twitter, this might be an untapped channel for your business.

20. Leverage employee talents. At many companies, the employees with the most effective social media presence do not necessarily work in the PR department. It could be somebody at the reception desk, employees in IT, or somebody working in the lunchroom. What if you could enlist their help, skills, and audience to help you promote your own business strategies and connect to new

stakeholders? How could every employee be a beacon for the company?

21. Integrate. Don't forget to promote your Twitter handle and relevant hashtags in ads, TV commercials, business cards, customer communications, and other marketing materials.

22. Encourage live tweeting. Encouraging employees and other stakeholders to tweet about the best moments from special events can help amplify your marketing messaging. You might even spend some time training employees on how to do this well.

23. Use Twitter as part of a social selling strategy. If you're trying to make new connections and form relationships that might result in a live meeting, the two best places to develop new leads (especially in a B2B environment) are Twitter and LinkedIn. Think about using some of the advanced search options to find new customers and connect with them.

24. Use Lead Generation Cards. One of Twitter's innovations is a "business card" that attaches to a sponsored tweet that allows you to collect contact information from those who want to learn more about your business. This data collection system integrates with most CRM systems.

25. And one last business idea—do *not* put a Twitter feed on your website. This is definitely something

not to do. Yes, it's cool. Yes, it's trendy. But it can backfire on you.

Done correctly, Twitter is lively, personal, and human. If you display your Twitter feed on your website, you're displaying one side of a two-sided conversation. It's conversation out of context. Why would you do this? What possible value could this create?

A couple of years ago, a friend asked me to review his website. When I went to his landing page, the thing that hit you right in the face was the word "PORNOGRAPHY" in the Twitter stream. In context, he was making a funny comment in response to a friend. On a website it sends the wrong message.

Everything communicates. Everything you say, and everything you don't say, reflects on your brand. "LOL!!!! You rock Tony!" and "Delayed in Dallas for the second time this week" are appropriate for a Twitter stream, but is that the right business communication you want to display on your company website?

Of course, if your Twitter stream is simply company links and press releases, you're safe. But you're also probably not too successful on Twitter.

So there you have it. A few of my favorite business ideas for Twitter. I know you're probably so excited to try some of these new ideas out that you can hardly wait to finish the book!

18

Tao Power: Putting It All Together

My premise has been that you are reading this book because you hope to gain some personal or business benefits from Twitter. We've covered a lot of ground, but I have one more important secret of success to share with you.

The greatest benefit Twitter provides is the new doors that are opened. But to realize the greatest opportunities, Twitter on its own is probably not enough. Let me explain what I mean.

Weak Links and Strong Links

I decided to go out to the folks in my Twitter audience one holiday season and ask them to support a charity I believe in. I had never done this before, and it was a surprisingly great success—I raised more than $6,000 in one week.

On one level, this was inspiring to me because I realized this could have never happened if I had not worked for years to build an engaged social media audience. Without question, Twitter enabled this achievement. But let's peel this back to learn another lesson about creating business benefits on Twitter.

My charitable request was tweeted by 446 different Twitter connections, but only 92 of them actually made a donation. So the reality is, 354 people encouraged others to donate without donating anything themselves. This is the big challenge with social media in general. The connections we build initially are "weak links." It might be easy to get somebody to read a blog post or help with a tweet, but it is very hard to move people to take a concrete action like opening a wallet. Many people make the mistake of equating a large Twitter following with influence . . . and this is just not the case.

Of the 92 people who donated, I had met 80 of them in real life. I had done the work to convert these "weak" Twitter connections into "strong" personal relationships. The average donation of my strong-link friends was $65. The average donation of my weak-link Twitter connections was $15.

This means that only 12 people on Twitter whom I personally did not know out of 70,000 followers (at the time) saw the tweet asking for help and did something about it.

That's a conversion rate of less than 0.02 percent, probably the least effective sales channel you could ever imagine.

As I said, Twitter opens the doors for you, but the real magic happens when you work to turn these wonderful opportunities into real-life relationships. Nothing builds true loyalty like calling a new Twitter friend in need, helping that friend over a cup of coffee, or looking the person up on a business trip to a new city.

Twitter and Regulated Industries

Once in a while I get pushback from businesses that operate in a highly regulated environment. Medical professionals, lawyers, financial managers, and defense contractors may have limitations on the information they can discuss in public. Remember, Twitter is a form of publishing.

And yet I believe most companies can find their Twitter happy place, even in a regulated industry. I met my friend Jeff Reed (@nvknow1) through a LinkedIn group. Jeff works as a wealth advisor for a large national company but had been hamstrung in his attempts to use social media.

"I am forbidden to use it," he told me. "The company is trying to figure out what to do, but in the meantime I feel like the world is passing me by."

Regulated industries like banks and healthcare have to pay attention to the legal ramifications of how they share information. The law is the law. Still, I think they are missing a bigger opportunity by not exploring how social media can be used on a very personal and human level.

I asked Jeff, "Does your company forbid you from attending a business networking meeting?"

"No."

"Do the people at your company keep you away from going to a chamber of commerce function?"

"No."

"When you go to these meetings, do they tell you what you can and can't say?"

"No," he laughed.

"Then what's the difference? This is just another business networking opportunity. You don't have to sell; you don't have to advise. You don't even have to identify your employer. Why not just be yourself, meet cool people, and learn from them? Who knows . . . they just might even turn into clients someday."

This got Jeff's attention. He was interested enough to enroll in one of my college classes, and from that point on he has been on fire with social networking. And it's working! He has even become an internal social media advisor to his own company. His company is creating competitive advantage through smart social media networking—even in a regulated industry.

A Case Study of Strong Connections

Let's bring all these ideas together through one last story.

One night when I was just starting out on Twitter, I was observing a conversation going back and forth between a woman named Amy Howell (@howellmarketing) and several marketing professionals in my tribe.

Amy seemed enthusiastic (used lots of !!!), supportive, intelligent, and fun. From her professional and complete Twitter profile, I could tell she ran a public relations and marketing firm in my home state of Tennessee. The link to her website also showed me that we share many interests and that she is a fellow blogger. Perhaps there were opportunities for business synergy?

Amy and I had connected—we were following each other on Twitter—but we had not really *connected*. She seemed like a person I would like to get to know and possibly even do business with. I needed to turn this weak link into a strong business relationship that would result in something. Over the next few weeks I . . .

- Looked for opportunities just to say hello and compliment her when I saw her online.
- Read her tweets and, when I saw interesting content, retweeted it to my followers.

- Started reading her blog, commented on it, and in an act of authentic helpfulness, tweeted links to her blog to the people who follow me. This helped promote her efforts and get me on her "radar screen."

Soon Amy and I were having regular conversations over Twitter. We grew to like each other, and she appreciated the support I gave her by tweeting her links and blog posts.

As I often do, I invited my new Twitter friend to talk on the phone. In this age of conversation avoidance, a phone call or visit on Skype seems like a luxury, but I think this is an essential part of building and cementing strong new business relationships, especially if a live meeting across the miles is improbable.

In our call Amy mentioned that she had an upcoming meeting in my hometown and that she wanted to stay overnight to have dinner with me and my wife. I couldn't have been more pleased and excited to finally meet my new friend.

But a conflict arose. I had committed to a speaking engagement at a regional marketing meeting, and the time of the event was moved to the exact day Amy was to be in town. I had an idea—wouldn't Amy make a great addition to the panel discussion? Everyone agreed, and Amy became an important part of the program, giving her the chance to network with a host of relevant business professionals.

She was so grateful for this important professional exposure and my authentic helpfulness.

After the event, we had dinner, and Amy mentioned that she was part of a professional group of fellow marketers and bloggers. The group was going to attend a conference together in Memphis and then meet afterward to discuss ways to work together. It sounded like fun, and shortly, through Amy's recommendation, I became part of the group.

On my way to Amy's Memphis meeting, I had to drive through Nashville during the traditional lunch hour and decided to reach out to a new Twitter friend named Laura Click (@lauraclick) who lived in that city. Although I did not know her very well, I invited her to meet for lunch since I was nearby.

Laura and I hit it off, and this lunch meeting started an important business relationship for me—Laura has since helped me with client writing assignments, contributed a guest blog post, helped me write a chapter for a book, and collaborated on a charity effort. She has become one of my most important business partners. As my business grew, I actually moved several of my customers over to her when she started her own consulting business, helping her jump-start her solo career.

When I arrived in Memphis, I had great fun meeting many Twitter friends face-to-face for the first time. One of them was Glen Gilmore (@glengilmore), a well-known

New Jersey attorney and one of Amy's strategic partners. Although Glen worked in a regulated industry, he had become a true social media expert. Months later I was in a position to recommend my new friend for a teaching position at his alma mater, Rutgers University—a thrill for both of us.

I also got to meet other marketing thought leaders like Billy Mitchell (@billymitchell1) and Anne Deeter Gallaher (@adgallaher), who have become close friends and business collaborators. Over the next few years, Billy, Anne, and Amy have all hired me for paid consulting, writing, and speaking assignments.

We developed such a close friendship that many of the people from that first meeting in Memphis started a marketing conference together called Social Slam, which has attracted more than 600 attendees annually. Amy and I continue to find business opportunities for each other and partner in many ways . . . and we always will.

None of this would have happened without the Tao power of connections, content, and helpfulness. This is how it works.

The Tao Movement

Since the first edition of this book was published, *The Tao of Twitter* has inspired thousands of readers and sparked countless new connections and business benefits. It is not just a book. It is a movement. And here we are at the end. You're part of it now, too!

By now I hope you can see this undeniable pattern of Targeted Connections, Meaningful Content, and Authentic Helpfulness running through every success story. And while it has created surprising and amazing benefits, in the long term the most important payoff for me will be the relationships I've formed with the many wonderful people I've mentioned, like Michelle Chmielewski Belcic, Aaron Killian, Amy Howell, and Tony Dowling, plus the hundreds of other folks who have followed the Tao of Twitter. It can happen for you, too.

I want to end this book the same way I end all my social media marketing classes—with a quote from a university student who left this comment on my blog:

> Social media marketing is not something that can be taught—It has to be experienced and this is why schools have a hard time teaching classes about it. Students who take advantage of social media will have a leg up on those who do not. Formal education and books can show you the tools . . . but it is up to YOU to learn how to apply them for you and your business.

I'm *so grateful* that you've read my book. But no matter how many times you return to it, you can't master the Tao of

Twitter until you immerse yourself in it and learn by doing. So I want to encourage you to be persistent, patient, and present.

Best of luck as you find your own path, your own Tao, on your lifetime Twitter adventure.

Notes

Chapter 2

1. Tragically, Trey died a few months after the first edition of this book was published. He loved *The Tao of Twitter* and this story of our collaboration so much that I decided to keep this case study in all future editions of this book as an everlasting tribute to his kindness and friendship.

Chapter 4

1. "Social Habit" research study conducted by Edison Research, Princeton, N.J.
2. http://www.businessinsider.com/twitter-destroys -facebook-2010-12.
3. http://www.emarketer.com/Article.aspx?R=1007639.
4. http://www.exacttarget.com/.

Chapter 5

1. http://firstmonday.org/htbin/cgiwrap/bin/ojs/index.php/ fm/article/view/2317/2063.

Chapter 6

1. If you're completely new to Twitter and unfamiliar with terms such as "direct message" or "Follow Friday," don't worry! These are explained in Chapter 8 under the section "Language of Twitter."

Chapter 9

1. http://gigaom.com/2010/04/30/the-short-and-illustrious -history-of-twitter-hashtags/.

Chapter 10

1. Some of these ideas came from my friend, entrepreneur, and blogger Neicole Crepeau.
2. Official List Set-up instructions courtesy Twitter website.

Acknowledgments

The story of any Twitter journey is one of friendships. I have dozens of wonderful tales about hundreds of people I could have included in this book. My love and deepest respect goes out to my Twitter tribe, students, and customers. You have changed my life in amazing ways.

To my offline family, Ryan, Lauren, Avery, and Hannah. Thank you for your support and patience while I was buried in my laptop. Your role in my life had nothing to do with Twitter.

My dear love Rebecca, the queen of my life—thank you!

Most important, I thank God for His patience with this broken servant and for granting me the opportunity to glorify Him through this work.

Index

Videos, 6, 67–68, 71–72, 146
Vine, 146

W
Website Cards,
  146–147
Websites, 42, 184–187

Wefollow.com, 48
Who to Follow gadget, 45
Winter Hockey Classic, 100

Y
Yahoo!, 155, 174
YouTube, 49

About the Author

Mark W. Schaefer is a globally recognized blogger, speaker, educator, business consultant, and author who blogs at [grow]—one of the top marketing blogs of the world.

Mark has worked in global sales, PR, and marketing positions for 30 years and now provides consulting services as Executive Director of U.S.-based Schaefer Marketing Solutions. He specializes in social media marketing training, and clients include both start-ups and global brands such as IBM, AT&T, Johnson & Johnson, and the U.S. Air Force.

Mark has advanced degrees in marketing and organizational development and holds seven patents. He is a faculty member of the graduate studies program at Rutgers University and is the author of three additional bestselling marketing books, *Return on Influence*, *Born to Blog*, and *Social Media Explained*.

He is among the world's most recognized social media authorities and has been a keynote speaker at conferences and universities around the world. Mark is a popular and entertaining commentator and has appeared on many national television shows and in periodicals including the *Wall Street Journal*, *Wired*, the *New York Times*, CNBC, and the CBS News.

Follow Mark on the Web
Blog: http://www.businessesGROW.com
Twitter: @markwschaefer
Facebook: http://on.fb.me/markwschaefer
LinkedIn: http://linkd.in/mwschaefer
YouTube: http://bit.ly/yt-schaefer
Podcast: http://bit.ly/marketingcompanion